# VIEWS FROM THE APACHE FRONTIER

# VIEWS FROM THE APACHE FRONTIER

# REPORT ON THE NORTHERN PROVINCES OF NEW SPAIN

by
José Cortés,
Lieutenant in the Royal Corps of Engineers,
1799

Edited by Elizabeth A.H. John
Translated by John Wheat

University of Oklahoma Press : Norman

By Elizabeth A. H. John

*Storms Brewed in Other Men's Worlds* (College Station, Texas, 1975; paperback, Lincoln, Nebraska, 1981)

*Views from the Apache Frontier* (Norman, 1989)

Library of Congress Cataloging-in-Publication Data

Cortés y de Olarte, José Maria, d. 1811.
[Memoria sobre las provincias del norte de Nueva España. English]
Views from the Apache frontier: report on the northern provinces
of New Spain / by José Cortés ; edited by Elizabeth A.H. John ;
translated by John Wheat. — 1st ed.
p. cm.
Translation of: Memorias sobre las provincias del norte de Nueva España.
Bibliography: p.
Includes index.
ISBN 978-0-8061-2609-8 (paper)

1. Apache Indians-History-Sources. 2. Indians of North
America-Southwest, New-History-Sources. 3. Southwest,
New-History-To 1848-Sources. 4. Texas-History-To
1846-Sources. 5. Mexico-History-Spanish colony, 1540-1810
-Sources. I. John, Elizabeth Ann Harper, 1928- . II. Title.
E99.A6C6413 1989
979'.00497-dc19                      88-40543
                     CIP

The paper in this book meets the guidelines for permanence and durability of the Committee on Production Guidelines for Book Longevity of the Council on Library Resources, Inc.

Copyright © 1989 by Elizabeth A. H. John. Published by the Univesity of Oklahoma Press, Norman, Publishing Division of the University. Manufactured in the U.S.A. Paperback published 1994.

# CONTENTS

V

# ILLUSTRATIONS

# MAPS

# EDITOR'S PREFACE

Lieutenant José María Cortés has taught me a great deal, directly and indirectly, since I chanced upon his work in May, 1979, during my first visit to the British Library. An extensive, unpublished eighteenth century treatment of Apaches seemed the least likely of finds in that institution's collection of Spanish manuscripts, which had long been famous and, I presumed, well studied. Indeed, even on first scan, parts of the Cortés commentary on Apache culture looked suspiciously familiar. But other parts were downright astonishing: the minutely detailed eyewitness account of a baffling ritual of cremation and purification, which was unlike anything I had ever seen in the literature on Apaches, and, scattered throughout, other descriptive data almost as novel. Equally remarkable was the author's sympathetic attitude toward the most notoriously troublesome aborigines on New Spain's northern frontier. Here was a Spanish military engineer contending in 1799, on the basis of personal observation and research, that Apaches actually loved peace, and that their occasional breaches of treaties were both defensible under natural law and fully warranted under rules of conduct employed by the most civilized powers.

No less intriguing was the broad scope of this book-length manuscript on the northern frontier of New Spain. Rather than addressing the Apachería as a narrow regional problem, Cortés considered it in the strategic global context of revolution and contest for empire. Here was a current analysis of the perennial, pervasive British threat to the Spanish empire, as well as an assessment, at once admiring and cautionary, of the new Anglo-American republic, with sophisticated emphasis on the demographic factors that made the United States so dangerous to Spain's interests in America.

Cortés also stressed the strategic importance of remote Indian worlds far beyond the Apachería. Although his personal experience had equipped him for detailed discussion only of Apaches, he sketched many more nations, not only in the northerly reaches of New Spain but also in Spain's vast province of Louisiana. Those sections of the report were conspicuously uneven: the coverage of Indians in Louisiana was reasonably accurate for the 1790s; that of Indians in Texas, garbled almost beyond comprehension. Then knowing little about the welter of little tribes in present Arizona and California, I could only wonder about that segment of the Cortés effort, but subsequent investigation showed it to contain the best data available in that era.

Whatever usefulness the Cortés data might or might not have for anthropologists, there seemed little doubt that this ambitious military engineer's report warrants historians' attention. At the very least, it summarizes the knowledge of Indians of the trans-Mississippi West that was available to Spanish officialdom in the dawn of the nineteenth century. It also provides a rare glimpse of a sophisticated Spaniard's grasp of the dangers boding the end of Spanish empire in America.

So began nearly a decade's involvement with the Cortés *Memorias*. The experience had just enough unexpected developments from time to time to make it impossible to abandon the sometimes frustrating project. Having obtained a microfilm of the manuscript for further study, I sought Lieutenant Cortés in Janet R. Fireman's study of the Spanish Royal Corps of Engineers, and found that she discussed his brief tour of duty on the northern frontier of New Spain, citing military records in Spain that held promise of fuller detail. From her perspective as an historian of the Spanish military experience in the Borderlands, Dr. Fireman had rated the Cortés *Memorias* naive about Apaches and thus of little importance, a judgment quite consistent with conventional wisdom. However, trends emerging in my own ethnohistorical research indicated that the Cortés work deserved more positive consideration. But would it merit publication? Since Dr. Fireman had cited a microfilm of the Cortés *Memorias* in Arizona, I wondered whether she or some other scholar of that region were already working with the document. In that case, I should pursue it no further.

Happily, that autumn's meeting of the Western History Association, at San Diego, gave me the opportunity to consult Dr. Fireman, now established at the Los Angeles County Museum of Natural History. She assured me that she had no further plans to work with the Cortés *Memorias* and would be interested to see what I might make of it. She had no idea why the University of Arizona happened to have that microfilm.

On the way home to Texas, I stopped in Tucson and learned from the Special Collections Department of the University of

Arizona's Library that no other investigator had prior claim on that copy of the manuscript. However, my call for the Cortés *Memorias* elicited not the expected microfilm, but a lavish collector's tome, quite unlike the austere, small, brown leather volume in the British Library. Here was a thick, quarto volume, bound in blue morocco, gilt-edged, its text beautifully lettered and embellished, with the slender Cortés report padded by the addition of the much longer Domínguez-Escalante diary to which Cortés had alluded. Now the Cortés *Memorias* would lead me into the fascinating, sometimes manic world of nineteenth-century bibliophiles whose collections became vitally important to historians of Hispanic America.

Describing the Cortés report to scholars with particular expertise on Apaches gave rise to other questions. Dr. Bernard L. Fontana, field historian at the University of Arizona Library, immediately pointed out that a newly published article presented a translation of another Spanish official's report, generated on the same frontier in the same decade, displaying conclusions strikingly unlike those argued by Cortés in his defense of the Apaches. Clearly, those contradictions would have to be addressed if the Cortés report were to be published.

Within weeks, a stint as ethnohistorical consultant on an Apache museum project at the University of Oklahoma gave me the opportunity to mention the Cortés report to the dean of Apache studies, Morris Opler. He assured me that the work was well known to anthropologists as a segment of the 1856 congressional report on explorations for a transcontinental railway route. But further discussion led both of us to recognize a wide discrepancy between the book-length manuscript that I described and the relatively brief data in the railway report. Certainly Professor Opler had never seen the account of the bizarre funeral witnessed by Cortés. To facilitate comparison with my microfilm, Professor Opler promptly furnished me a duplicate of his own photocopy of the Cortés material from the congressional report. I soon ascertained that the material published in the congressional report comprised only brief excerpts of the Cortés *Memorias*, omitting its meatiest material on Apache culture. When I reported that to Professor Opler, his encouraging interest ended any lingering doubt that the entire report should be published.

Since I was scheduled to visit Spain in the summers of 1983 and

1985, I added the search for Cortés and his work to my research agenda for those trips. Meanwhile, visits to Mexico and to various repositories in this country turned up other fragments of the puzzle. Now it was essential to examine the contradictions between the Cortés report and the recently published report of a contemporary in the Spanish service.

It was soon obvious that the conflicting report could not have been written by the official to whom the article attributed it. Since the published translation derived from a manuscript in the Museo Naval, I investigated the question of its authorship on my 1983 visit to Madrid. In the Museo Naval's manuscript collection I found enough clues to develop two alternative hypotheses of the author's identity, which I rashly published, only to learn later that both were wrong. More important was the puzzling discovery that the viewpoint of the manuscript in the Museo Naval seemed to agree closely with that of Cortés. Taking home a microfilm of the Museo Naval manuscript for close comparison, I found that the apparent contradictions stemmed from glaring errors of both commission and omission in the published translation. The mere note that I had intended to write concerning the false attribution of the manuscript would not suffice; to quash the issue of contradictions between that report and the Cortés *Memorias*, it would be necessary to publish a complete new translation. Fortunately, it was a responsible professional journal that had suffered the mishap of the misleading translation, and as soon as its staff could verify the accuracy of my submission, it published the corrective translation, only a year and a half after I discovered the discrepancy in Madrid.[1]

While that clarification smoothed the way for publication of the book-length Cortés manuscript, translating the much shorter document for publication taught me just how grueling and time-consuming such a task could be. John Wheat, translator of the Béxar Archives at the Barker Texas History Center at the University of Texas, lent invaluable support, helping me sort out thorny patches in that very rough little manuscript, and verifying the whole before it went on to the journal for final verification by specialists there. That experience reinforced my longstanding appreciation of John's sensitivity to historical context as well as his superior competence in Spanish and his exacting standards of translation. Confident that John could translate the much longer Cortés manuscript far more expeditiously than I, and with the polish that the scholarly Cortés deserves, I asked that he collaborate on this project as translator. Thanks to John's agreement, this volume appears sooner and reads better than could otherwise have occurred.

Both of us learned much from our cordial collaborative enterprise. Once John prepared the translation, we checked it against the microfilm together, particularly alert for instances where the usual interpretation of the Spanish text might have missed a special meaning peculiar to the historical or anthropological context. We found enough cases to justify our concern about risks inherent in translating without access to essential background information. John's grasp of niceties of construction preserved the literary style of Cortés as I could never have done, stressing fidelity in tone as well as meaning. That emphasis is crucial in a work imbued with such passion and agony as Cortés invested in this unusual manuscript.

Some readers may find bothersome the many variations in the spelling of proper names, which are presented as they appear in the manuscript. Retaining the disparate spellings serves the purposes of ethnohistorical and linguistic analysis by demonstrating in original context the many forms that Indian nomenclature takes in the documentary record. It is essential in this instance because the overwhelming confusion of Cortés regarding Texas Indians resulted from the wildly varied spellings that he found in his documentary research. Having necessarily eschewed standardization of the names of Indian peoples, we also deemed it appropriate generally to preserve the manuscript's rendition of place names. Therefore, this text displays the exotic forms in which some Anglo-American place names filtered across the language barrier. To preserve the emphases of Cortés, we have also retained some capitalizations that defy current editorial standards. The system of numbering parts, sections, and paragraphs is that employed by Cortés to shape his diverse data into some semblance of a scientific report.

My primary concern as editor was to elucidate the circumstances from which this unusual work arose, with particular emphasis on the qualifications and the probable purposes of Cortés. Identifying the sources of his information proved especially rewarding because it afforded a glimpse of the documentary holdings of the Commandancy General of the Internal Provinces at Chihuahua, an archive whose early nineteenth-century dispersal and subsequent loss has sorely impeded historical investigation of the Hispanic Borderlands. Investigating the arena in which Cortés served also provided glimpses of the communities on the northern frontier in which the young officer developed his own appreciation of native peoples and presidial soldiers. Such background material comprises the Introduction.

The search for possible results of the Cortés report led back to beleaguered Spain in the era of the Napoleonic Wars and turned up personal as well as national tragedy. Tracing the fate of the *Memorias* beyond the author's time dramatized the turbulence—desperate at worst, random at best—through which manuscripts too often toss before reaching the secure repositories in which scholars find them. Such matters comprise the Epilogue.

Still, the Introduction and Epilogue only frame the heart of the matter, which is the translated *Memorias* of Cortés. To minimize intrusion between twentieth-century reader and eighteenth-century author, annotation is largely limited to necessary identifications of Indian groups, individuals, flora, fauna, places, and events. Given the unevenness of the Cortés work, which reflects the great variations in the nature of his sources and his subject matter, the extent and character of the annotation vary correspondingly. Some pertinent controversies and conflicting interpretations in the scholarly literature are noted, and there are some suggestions for further reading.

But first, I suggest that you let the vigorous argument of Cortés himself sweep you along, with the notes interrupting you no more than is really necessary to your comprehension of his text. Find out how the northern frontier of New Spain seemed in 1799 to an intelligent observer who cared passionately about Spain's role in the New World and about the native peoples. Then come back to the editorial notes if you wish to see how his effort meshes with current understanding.

Of course, even so zealous a sympathizer as Cortés could not convey the Apaches' point of view, and there are no Apache documents from that era to balance the Spanish perspective. But in this century some Apache artists have depicted details of their people's traditional lifeways in works that display the Apaches' sense of themselves. The most distinguished body of such art is that of Allan Houser (Ha-o-zous), a Chiricahua-Fort Sill Apache whose work is particularly appropriate to this book because the Apaches whom Cortés observed most closely were Chiricahuas.

Houser, a great-grandson of noted Chief Mangas Coloradas, was among the first children born to the Chiricahua band at Fort Sill after their release from twenty-seven years of captivity as prisoners of war.[2] His father, Sam Haozous, born in 1868, had learned the old life of the Apachería in boyhood, before the family was caught up in the last desperate episodes of resistance led by his uncle, Geronimo, and he carefully preserved the traditions of his people through their long captivity from 1886 to 1912. Although he and his wife adapted admirably to the farmer's life assigned to Apaches in Oklahoma by the U.S. government, Sam Haozous diligently taught his children the oral traditions of their people, rearing them in the spirit of traditional Apache beliefs and customs. When his son, Allan, began painting scenes of the old Apache life, Haozous monitored the details in order that their lifeways be shown correctly. Hence the special documentary significance of the well-instructed son's paintings. Nine of the ten Houser paintings reproduced throughout this book depict aspects of Apache culture discussed by Cortés. The tenth, *Apache Herdsman*, shows a contemporary aspect of Apache life that accords with the expectations of Cortés regarding their peaceful future.

Since earning initial recognition as a painter, Houser has won still greater international fame as a sculptor whose extraordinarily beautiful, sophisticated works evoke the timeless spirituality of Apaches and occasionally of such neighboring peoples as Navajos and Pueblos. Those dimensions of Apache life were beyond the ken of Cortés, but their contemporary expressions by Houser harmonize with the Spanish engineer's sense of Apache potential.

The Cortés map reproduced in the Editor's Introduction is of much less satisfactory quality than either the publisher or I would wish, since the physical peculiarities of the original–described in the Introduction–make it virtually impossible to reproduce intelligibly. However, it seems unthinkable to omit from this volume the map that Cortés prepared to accompany his *Memorias*, and this reproduction should at least give an idea of the scope as well as the surprising crudeness of the effort. The architectural drawings by Cortés, which are reproduced here in the Epilogue, surely give a fairer impression of the draftsmanship of Cortés. Other illustrations herein show the rather handsome style of the earliest known version of the Cortés manuscript, from which this book derives. Cartographer John V. Cotter, of Austin, prepared the maps for this volume from data compiled by the editor.

This book owes much to the supportive interest of fellow scholars of history and anthropology. I am especially indebted to Professor Opler, who was instrumental in convincing me that this work should be done and generous in consultation. He also recommended the project at a very early stage to the attention of the University of Oklahoma Press. Dr. Fontana, who read the manuscript for the publisher, generously supplied well-documented suggestions that greatly strengthened the final product. Dr. Fireman, who pioneered the study of the Royal Engineers in the Borderlands, also read the manuscript for the publisher and made helpful suggestions.

The endeavor drew upon the patient cooperation of many librarians and archivists in Madrid, Segovia, Simancas, Seville, and Cádiz, in Spain, as well as in the British Library, to which I returned in 1986 to clear up questions that had emerged since I first encountered the *Memorias* there in 1979. In Mexico City, I incurred still further debts of gratitude to archivists and librarians, and to the many citizens who responded helpfully to my search for the site of a building designed by Cortés. In this country, manuscript specialists at the New York Public Library, the Library of Congress, the Bancroft Library, and the University of Arizona Library were unstinting in their help. At home I relied principally upon the superb resources and excellent staff of the Benson Latin American Collection at the University of Texas.

Finally, let me express my appreciation to Peter W. M. John. An extraordinarily supportive husband, he was my helpful companion on much of the travel that this project entailed, and remains at home an indispensable bulwark against the computer's occasional treachery.

ELIZABETH A. H. JOHN

*Austin, Texas*

# VIEWS FROM THE APACHE FRONTIER

# EDITOR'S INTRODUCTION

What drove a lieutenant, not yet thirty years old, to produce such an extraordinary document as these *Memorias*? That such a perceptive and concerned officer as José María Cortés should report his observations of a chronically troublesome frontier was to be expected, especially from one of the elite Royal Corps of Engineers. But Cortés went much further, elaborating his firsthand experiences on the northern frontier of New Spain through personal consultations and archival research, and casting his results in a broad geopolitical framework that might seem presumptuous in so junior an officer. Besides the pride and passionate love of nation that pervade the work and the manifest intellectual drive of Cortés, some personal ambition must also have figured in his remarkable effort.[1]

Cortés indeed had good reason to expect sympathetic interest in the *Memorias* at high levels. The head of the corps—the *ingeniero general*—was then the distinguished Gen. José de Urrutia, who had made his own substantial mark on the record of New Spain's northern frontier three decades earlier. When the Marqués de Rubí, assisted by Capt. Nicolás de Lafora of the royal engineers, toured the northern provinces on the epoch-making inspection of 1766-67, the cartographer assigned to the expedition was José de Urrutia, then a *subteniente* in the Regiment of America. Urrutia's precisely drawn plans and elevations of each of the presidios, together with his maps of some frontier towns, became treasures of the cartography of New Spain.[2] In the 1790s, Urrutia won recognition as one of Spain's most successful field commanders. But somehow the distinguished general incurred the displeasure of the powerful Minister Manuel de Godoy and, perhaps as a result, found himself shunted away from field command to head the Royal Corps of Engineers.[3] Cortés would make certain that Urrutia personally received a copy of his *Memorias*, whether through the official channels of distribution or outside them.[4]

However complex and subtle the author's motives, suffice it now to understand these *Memorias* as the fruit of a propitious convergence of several forces in the wilds of northern New Spain: the inquisitive, well-trained mind of Cortés; the special fascination of close encounter with Apaches; the mind-boggling multiplicity of native peoples, at once so threatening and so promising for God and King; the cumulative experience of veterans readily accessible to the visiting officer; the archives replete with two and a half centuries' reportage on remote peoples and places; and the young officer's compelling sense of multiple crises looming over the Spanish Americas.

José María Cortés y de Olarte was a native of Tarifa, on the southernmost tip of Spain. His odyssey began in the spring of 1785, with his enlistment in the Regiment of Toledo as a fifteen-year-old cadet, i.e., a volunteer serving in expectation of a commission, but his destiny lay with the select Royal Corps of Engineers. For the requisite preparation in mathematics, Cadet Cortés crossed the Strait of Gibraltar to Céuta, in Morocco, where he studied in the royal military academy. Three years as a student in that strategic bastion of Spain on the North African shore must have afforded Cortés his first opportunities to observe Spanish management of alien, sometimes hostile, peoples beyond Iberia, a useful preliminary to service on the Crown's North American frontier.

In January, 1789, Cortés won his commission as *subteniente* (second lieutenant) and at the same time the rank of *ayudante de ingenieros* (assistant engineer) in the Royal Corps of Engineers.[5] He then served in his native Andalusia until March, 1793, when he was assigned to Galicia. After little more than a year's service in Spain's misty green northwest, in May, 1794, Cortés received his promotion to *teniente* (lieutenant) and *ingeniero extraordinario* (special engineer), with a posting to New Spain on special assignment to the Interior Provinces. Assignment to the Americas entailed at least five years' service, with no assurance of speedy relief afterward and a worrisome possibility of adverse effects on one's seniority in the corps.[6] Cortés was probably as displeased as any other ambitious officer with such a disadvantageous assignment, which may explain why he tarried in Spain more than a year after receiving the order. Not until May, 1795, did Cortés sail from Cádiz for Veracruz, whence he traveled via the viceregal capital in Mexico City to the *villa* of Chihuahua in Nueva Vizcaya, the headquarters of the Commandancy General of the Interior Provinces.[7]

There Cortés had the good fortune to serve under the able, experienced Brig. Pedro de Nava, who served as commandant general of the Interior Provinces from 1790 to 1802 and was sympathetically supportive of the succession of engineers assigned to his command. Better still, the responsibilities of Cortés for engineering matters at various presidios required interaction with Lt. Col. Antonio Cordero y Bustamante, the most distinguished of all presidial commanders, who was then serving as commandant inspector of troops in the Interior Provinces, second in rank only to Nava. In his quarter century of service on the northern frontier, Cordero had gained not only great military repute but also extensive knowledge of the native peoples and considerable skill in dealing with them.

Within a few months after Cortés arrived on the northern frontier, in 1796, Cordero was appointed governor of the province of Coahuila.[8] Perhaps it was Cordero's impending move from Nueva Vizcaya to Coahuila that led Commandant General Nava to order that most expert of all his officers to summarize his knowledge of Apaches. At the very least, the document would form an invaluable guide for Nava and his subordinates in dealing with the various Apache groups; perhaps it would also enlighten those higher authorities who wrestled with issues of policy involving Apaches. Whatever Nava's purpose, Cordero's report[9] made a tremendous impression upon the newly arrived Lieutenant Cortés, who eventually drew heavily upon it for the treatment of Apaches in his own *Memorias*.

Although Cortés served three years and five months in the Interior Provinces, the only specific report of his movements is his own remark that in October and November, 1797, he was on special commission at the presidio of Janos. However, Cortés had visited Janos before, in the course of his routine inspections of the presidios of the commandancy general. His report to the commandant general concerning the structure of Janos cast doubt on the repeated representations of its new commandant, Capt. Manuel Rengel, about ruinous conditions there and on his unauthorized expenditures for "emergency" repairs. Rengel's assessment had been surprising, given that the highly capable Cordero had been the commandant of Janos through much of the previous decade, but Nava acquiesced until he received the contradicting engineer's report. Then, in the autumn of 1797, Nava notified the Janos commandant of the discrepancy between his reports and the expert assessment of engineer Cortés, expressing astonishment at Rengel's repeated displays of ignorance concerning military structures. Nava would send Lieutenant Cortés back to Janos forthwith, to examine thoroughly the buildings that Rengel had most recently proposed to rebuild. The commandant must show Cortés the breakdowns and ruins of which he had complained, so that Cortés could assess the actual needs for repair and propose suitable remedies, with cost estimates. Rengel would have to convince Cortés; Nava would accept no new representations on the subject once Cortés left Janos.[10]

Hence the opportunity of Cortés for an extended second visit to Janos, which Cordero had made one of the liveliest hubs of interaction with Apaches. Moreover, the chaplain at Janos was the doughty Fray Francisco Atanasio Domínguez. Little more than twenty years before, in the company of fellow Franciscan Fray Silvestre Vélez de Escalante, Father Domínguez had ventured farther among the indigenous peoples northwestward from New Mexico than any Europeans before them or for decades afterward.[11] Cortés had already studied the summary of their diary when he met Father Domínguez at Janos, and must have been all the more impressed to hear the earnest enthusiasm with which the venerable priest spoke of those remote, mostly welcoming peoples whom he had so longed to garner to the Catholic faith. Surely his discussions with Father Domínguez helped determine that Cortés would consider the Apachería in the larger context of Indian peoples northward, eastward, and westward.

Still, the immediate fascination for Cortés was the Apaches. Making the most of his opportunities to observe them directly as well as to learn from veterans of the frontier service, the young engineer grew from sympathetic inquiry to virtual advocacy. By the late eighteenth century, Spaniards of the northern frontier knew Apaches in diverse roles: as vengeful foes and rapacious raiders; as allies, indispensable scouts, guides, and couriers; as denizens, often uncertain, of presidial settlements and occasionally of mission communities; as peaceful traders and sometimes poachers.

The contradictions posed an intolerable dilemma for the Spanish Crown. However useful the peaceful Apaches made themselves, the Interior Provinces could not thrive as long as Apache marauders plagued them. In 1786, New Spain's Viceroy Bernardo de Gálvez, who had served briefly on the Apache frontier as a young captain, sought definitive resolution of the "Apache problem." The new guidelines that he promulgated were at once sympathetic and toughminded.[12] Apaches were to be given every opportunity and incentive to settle peacefully in the vicinity of designated presidios near their homelands, with subsidies to offset loss of their livelihood by raiding. Relentless, systematic war would be waged against those who clung to the predatory lifestyle.

Gálvez died too soon to see his plan implemented, but a cadre of experienced, dedicated officers on the northern frontier pursued it into the next century with considerable success. While the pacification program never embraced all Apaches, enough of them settled peacefully at the designated presidios to validate the concept. At Janos, Cortés saw one of the most successful of communities of *Apaches de paz*, and he presumably observed other such *establecimientos de paz* at various presidios in Nueva Vizcaya, Sonora, and Coahuila to which his duties took him.[13] At the same time, some of those presidios were bases for intensive military campaigns designed to scour from their homelands all Apaches who persisted in raiding and warfare, so Cortés also had ample opportunity to note the circumstances of Apache warfare.

Commandant General Nava required his officers to learn as much as possible of Apache customs, and expected all members of the presidial companies to learn the Apache language. He wanted Apache friendship fostered in every practicable way: through consistently courteous, patient, fair treatment at every level; through frequent conferences of Spanish officers with Apache leaders; through the officers' cultivation of personal friendship with Apache individuals; through extended visits to Apache camps by competent, trustworthy interpreters. While the realities must have fallen short of Nava's counsel of perfection, Cortés could not have wished a more congenial official climate in which to study Apaches. Moreover, Cortés may have been predisposed toward sympathetic interest in the *Apaches de paz* program because of earlier exposure to the well-established *Moros de paz* program, which had functioned successfully for several decades around Spanish presidios in North Africa.[14]

In September, 1798, the Crown ordered Cortés back to Mexico City. By November, 1799, he had reported for duty in the viceregal capital, from which Viceroy Miguel José de Azanza forwarded to the king with his approval the petition of Cortés for four hundred pesos' reimbursement for the extraordinary expenses incurred in his travels to and from the Interior Provinces.

Sometime during that year of 1799, Cortés found time to complete his *Memorias sobre las provincias del norte de Nueva España*, a manuscript of 142 folios. One surviving copy says that it was completed on May 3, 1799. Undoubtedly Cortés had already accomplished most of his research at Chihuahua in the rich archive of the commandancy general.[15] There he studied the diary of the Domínguez-Escalante expedition and the journal of Fray Francisco Garcés, documents that scholars still analyze as the ethnohistoric baseline for peoples of the Great Basin and the lower Colorado River basin.[16] Since those 1776 documents would remain the most complete, if not indeed the sole, reportage of their arenas for almost a century, Cortés rendered an important service in reducing their data to more organized, concise form. His effort concerning Texas was much less successful. While the reports of Fray Juan Morfi and of Lt. Col. Athanase de Mézières, also dating from the 1770s, were impressive summaries of that decade's knowledge of the Indians of Texas, the rest of the century brought extensive interaction between Spaniards and Indians in that arena and, consequently, much more knowledge. Hence, in the matter of Texas Indians, Cortés unluckily relied on outdated sources and, even worse, garbled them rather badly. Happily for his treatment of the Indians of Louisiana, the commandancy archive contained a concise, well-organized report that had been compiled at New Orleans in 1785 specifically for the use of the commandant general and remained essentially valid when Cortés used it a dozen years later.

While it is clear that most of the historical documentation was available in Chihuahua, it seems unlikely that such a remote frontier capital would have had the surprisingly up-to-date and largely accurate information about the United States and about events and publications in Europe and in remote reaches of North America that Cortés displayed in his *Memorias*. Surely some of that material had to be gleaned from the more extensive and current resources of Mexico City.

To illustrate his *Memorias* Cortés created a rough map of its principal arena, which is also dated 1799. It is uncertain whether the sole surviving copy, now in the British Library,[17] is actually the handiwork of Cortés or merely a tracing, perhaps made in the next decade at Cádiz for the collection of the renowned geographer Felipe Bauzá. Measuring fifty-five inches east to west and forty-six inches north to south, it was drawn on thin tracing paper, then

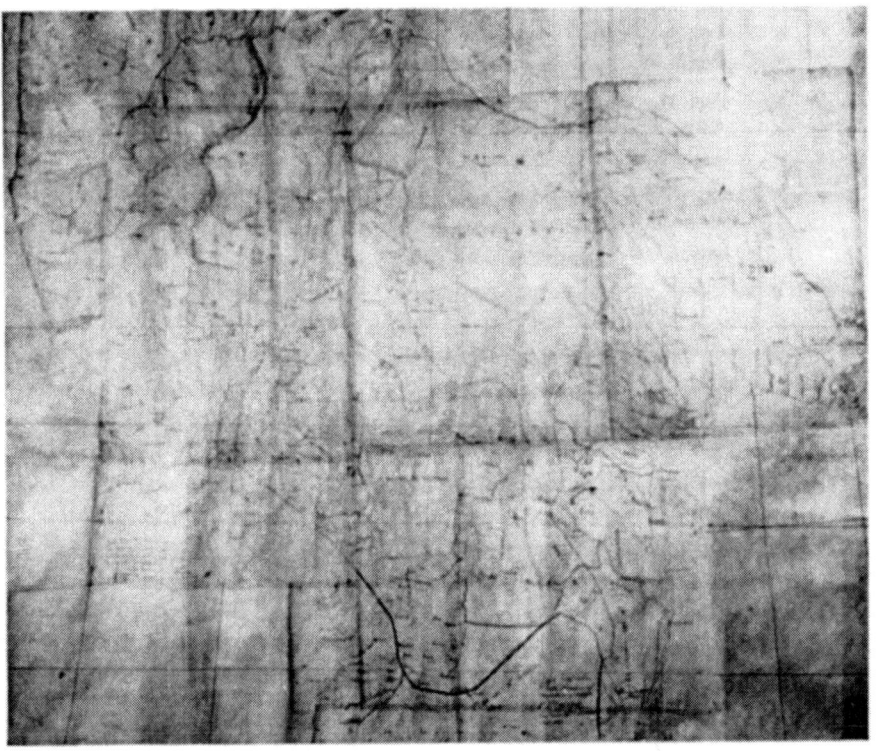

*Map of part of North America, augmented and corrected by Don José Cortés, Engineer of the Royal Armies.* 1799. Add. Ms. 17653c. (Reproduced by permission of the British Library.)

laminated onto drawing paper, which was subsequently laminated onto a heavier paper backing. Its incompleteness underscores the likelihood that the British Library's copy is a later, somewhat incomplete tracing of the original: the Moquis, who figure importantly in the *Memorias*, do not appear on the map; the presidial symbol at the location of Janos stands unlabeled, an unlikely omission for Cortés, who pinpointed Janos as a key post for his observation of Apaches. Streams and mountains appear roughly sketched in with pencil, and some were never inked over to match the rest of the map.

Whatever the history of the extant version, the map is an interesting reflection of this scholarly engineer's understanding of the northern frontier theater. Running in latitude from about 23° to 38° north and in longitude 258° to 286° from the meridian of Tenerife, its southernmost landmark is Zacatecas. Its easternmost feature is the Atchafalaya River flowing into the Mississippi Delta; its westernmost, the Colorado River flowing into the Gulf of California. On the northern rim of the map, the Río Grande dwindles into nothingness not far above Taos, in the mountains occupied by the Jicarillas, and just across the mountains westward the Colorado de California begins its westerly-southwesterly course to the gulf. The northeasternmost feature is the Red River—labeled Río Colorado de Nachitoches—which turns westward much too far north of Natchitoches and runs much too far west, into the mountains of New Mexico, suggesting that Cortés, like most of his contemporaries, confused the Red and Canadian rivers. Within Texas the label Colorado de las cañas distinguishes that major Texas river from the Colorados de California and de Nachitoches. All Texas rivers between the San Antonio and the Red are shown running sharply north-south, reflecting another common misconception that was not corrected until another officer in the Spanish service, Juan Pedro Walker, began mapping the Interior Provinces in the next decade.[18]

As might be expected of an officer whose primary responsibility was fortifications, Cortés displays the military posts in accurate detail. But the most enduring interest of his map today lies in its placement of various Indian peoples. The map reflects exactly the organization of the *Memorias*: the sector labeled *Naciones Apaches* is its central focus, flanked on the right by the sector of the *Naciones Orientales* and on the left by that of the *Naciones Occidentales*. Cortés prudently refrained from extending his map so far north as to encompass the peoples of the Missouri River or those of the Great Basin whom he treated in the *Memorias* on the basis of reports from traders and missionaries. Of those regions he could have drawn only vague conjectures.

The ambitious sweep of the *Memorias* reflects not only a zealous young officer's anxiety about imminent threats to the Crown's American patrimony but also his concern, in common with many informed Spaniards then and now, that the world understand more fully and fairly Spain's historical role in the Americas. Cortés had grown up in an era of great Spanish historical enterprise sparked by such concerns. Twenty years before Cortés wrote his *Memorias*, Carlos III had established the Archive of the Indies at Seville and charged distinguished scholar Juan Bautista Muñoz y Ferrandis to gather and organize all materials on the Americas in order to write an exhaustively documented history of the New World. In 1779 both Crown and academicians deemed it urgently necessary to refute the many inaccuracies recently propagated in foreign publications on the history of the Americas.[19] They also wished to counteract the sixteenth-century propaganda of crusading cleric Bartolomé de las Casas, which had not only sparked great reforms in the treatment of Indians in his own time but still colored foreigners' perceptions of Spanish America. Unfortunately, death overtook Muñoz at Madrid in the summer of 1799, when he had compiled 107 volumes of manuscript materials but had published only the first volume of his *Historia del Nuevo Mundo*, covering the period from discovery to 1500.[20]

Meanwhile, the Crown had demanded an analogous effort in New Spain. In response to a royal order of February 21, 1790, Viceroy Conde de Revillagigedo commissioned Father Miguel Vega, who in two years and four months of prodigious labor produced thirty-two manuscript volumes entitled *Colección de Memorias de Nueva España*. A collection of copies of old original documents and some contemporary ones for the history of Spanish North America, it was produced in triplicate, one copy remaining with the viceregal apparatus in Mexico City, one shipped to the Secretary of the Indies on December 31, 1792, and one carried to Spain by Revillagigedo himself after his term ended in 1794.[21]

In the midst of Father Vega's labors, a detachment from Alejandro Malaspina's Royal Scientific Expedition also searched archives in New Spain for materials of scientific, historic, and political interest. During the summer of 1791, while Malaspina's natural scientist Antonio Pineda y Ramírez pursued fieldwork in the hinterland, his younger brother, Arcadio Pineda, remained in Mexico City, gathering numerous reports that ranged from those of the Coronado expedition of the 1540s to some written in the current decade.[22]

Lieutenant Cortés, following Father Vega and Arcadio Pineda within seven years, must have been encouraged by the great display of official interest in the kinds of documents that he had used in Chihuahua. If he briefly continued such research in the vast archives at Mexico City, he must also have found his own inquiries considerably facilitated by the recent activity.

While Cortés reaped decidedly uneven results from his documentary research, the zealous engineer rendered a notable service in organizing data reported over a quarter century by the closest observers of New Spain's farthest frontier peoples. But the real meat of his *Memorias* is the matter of the Apaches, the crux of his effort, to which Cortés brought personal observation as well as superior primary sources. Not only did he have at Chihuahua the Cordero report, reflecting a quarter century of a superb officer's direct experience on the Apache frontier. It appears that Cortés also had access in Mexico City to a brief, roughly drafted memorandum in which the late Viceroy Bernardo de Gálvez expounded the understanding of Apaches that he had gleaned from his own early experience on the northern frontier and that he employed in 1786 in his definitive policy on Apaches.[23] Surely the farsighted viceroy would have been pleased that the *Memorias* of Cortés presented informed sympathy for the Apaches in the context of the larger forces bearing upon the far northern frontier. Twentieth-century scholars may well deem Cortés remiss in failing to acknowledge his substantial debt to other reports on the Apaches, especially that of Cordero on which he drew so freely. But that lapse is surely offset by the extraordinary usefulness to historians and anthropologists of his result: preservation of the most closely informed, best organized understanding of Apaches available at the end of the eighteenth century.

Quite apart from their ethnohistorical importance, these *Memorias* merit attention as a fragment of intellectual history. Cortés, born in the eleventh year of the enlightened reign of Carlos III and commissioned only a month after that sovereign's death, rode the wave of the Enlightenment in Spain. Although Cortés and his confreres suffered in Carlos IV a grievously inadequate monarch, the intellectual momentum of the Spanish Enlightenment did not soon decline. That the scholarly Cortés was very much at home in that milieu is evident in his *Memorias*, which display the emphasis upon system and analysis that characterized Enlightenment thought. Certainly the spirit of the Enlightenment shows in the admiration that Cortés expresses for the new republic of the United States, even as he warns against its threat to his own nation. But if the literature of the

French Enlightenment had ever inclined Cortés toward the "noble savage" concept of aborigines, his experience of Indians on the northern frontier of New Spain led him to more balanced, albeit still sympathetic, conclusions. In fact, his modernity notwithstanding, the Cortés commentary on the Apaches strikingly resembles two-thousand-year-old descriptions of Celtiberian tribes written by Roman officers struggling to subdue and Romanize those native peoples of Spain in much the same ways that Spanish officers strove to subdue and Hispanicize those of northern New Spain.

If the commentary of Cortés on the Apaches conjures up the fabric of ancient Spain, another of his themes mirrors one of the liveliest concerns in the renascent Spain of the 1980s. His attack upon the problem of the "Black Legend" of Spanish cruelty, which has so long warped international perceptions of Spain's role in the Americas, could well have been written by a scholarly Spanish patriot today.[24] A key manifestation of such contemporary concern is the probing, healing thrust of the emerging Columbian Quincentenary celebration. Vigorous Spanish leadership has sparked wide-ranging investigation of the encounter of New and Old Worlds, an international effort engaging the cooperation of scholars and officials throughout the Western Hemisphere and in some European nations as well. Given that national catastrophe thwarted the usefulness of his *Memorias* in his own time, Cortés could hardly have wished a more propitious moment than now to present his construction of the matters of the New World.

Consider, then, these *Memorias* as the world view of an exemplary young Spanish officer at the crest of the eighteenth-century Enlightenment—what he knew, what he thought, what he felt.

# MEMORIAS

## SOBRE LAS PROVINCIAS

## DEL

## NORTE DE NUEVA ESPAÑA

### POR

## D. JOSÉ CORTÉS, TENIENTE

### DEL REAL CUERPO

### DE YNGENIEROS.

## AÑO DE MDCCXC. IX.

Folio 2, Title Page, Cortés *Memorias*, Add. Ms. 17652. (Reproduced by permission of the British Library.)

# Report on the
# Northern Provinces of New Spain

by
Don José Cortés,
Lieutenant in the Royal Corps of Engineers

1799

# PREFACE[1]

There is such a common tendency among everyone to write and treat of foreign topics, ignoring the infinite objectives that, for greater personal enlightenment and service to the nation, should be the main points on which to focus their learning and knowledge, that what is no more than a faulty propensity assumes the nature of a passion. This consideration occupied my imagination when I entered into the farthest provinces of the king in North America, as well as the fact that only Spanish scholars may justly speak about the West Indies, a vital task in which their illustrious talents will never flag. Having established this proper notion, I recalled everything that had been written about the New World. With the exception of the conquests of Mexico, Peru, and Chile, and some other treatises with scientific notes and reports of oddities, the rest is quite meager and full of legend. We must believe that this is the cause of the ignorance and errors from which we suffer with regard to the true knowledge of what pertains to our American possessions. The lack of information and ideas on this point is so widespread that in Mexico and the other provinces of the king of New Spain the people speak with as much ignorance about the regions immediately to the north as they might about Constantinople.

The determination to disabuse the nation in this matter—as well as the hope that it might recognize intrinsically the great interests linking our peninsula with America, and the fact that, were the latter discovered without being possessed by the former, the Spanish monarchy would have been confined to a very meager territory—is a proposition that would easily demonstrate the public wisdom of expeditions by a commission of scholars devoted to such an elevated purpose. There has been much discussion and argument that Spain would be happier without the possession of America—grave delusion!—and we must consider the argument as one of those which, far from obscuring the truth, spread its rays and make it brighter and more resplendent. If God, the universal mover of all things, had not lifted the curtain hiding that great portion of the world from us, there would be a very controversial problem whether or not it would serve the grandeur and opulence of the Spanish nation to extend its sovereignty beyond the Atlantic. But now that its existence is known, and a direct and easy route to it has been discovered, it is one of the prime national interests that America be in our possession and not in that of France or England, to whom it probably would belong. Clearly, knowledge of America is a science which must be learned on the most solid principles understood by wise men and good compatriots.

After a personal struggle with my own lack of education and talents, I finally resolved to write what seemed to me most worthy and compatible with my limited capacities. Though my will ran free, it was overcome by the aforementioned reason and the concern that I might not finish in time. Thus I have not achieved the extended treatment which I proposed, it being limited by the journey I am about to undertake to the new post to which His Majesty sends me.[2]

The three parts into which this report on the northern provinces of New Spain is divided would provide a productive scholar with ample material to create an instructive, portentous, and fascinating work. I have not devoted myself to writing for this purpose, but rather with the spirit of fulfilling one of my prescribed duties, which, together with my natural character, compel me to the finest exactitude. Had I departed from that, I might present an entertaining and marvelous narrative, highlighting the rare and singular, and filling in with the aid of caprice and invention the gaps to be found in each section, so as to pursue a perfect order in the chapters and periods. But I could not help but confine myself to what I have seen, to my observations, to my reflections, and to the most scrupulous verification of all information that should be accepted with the mark of truth.

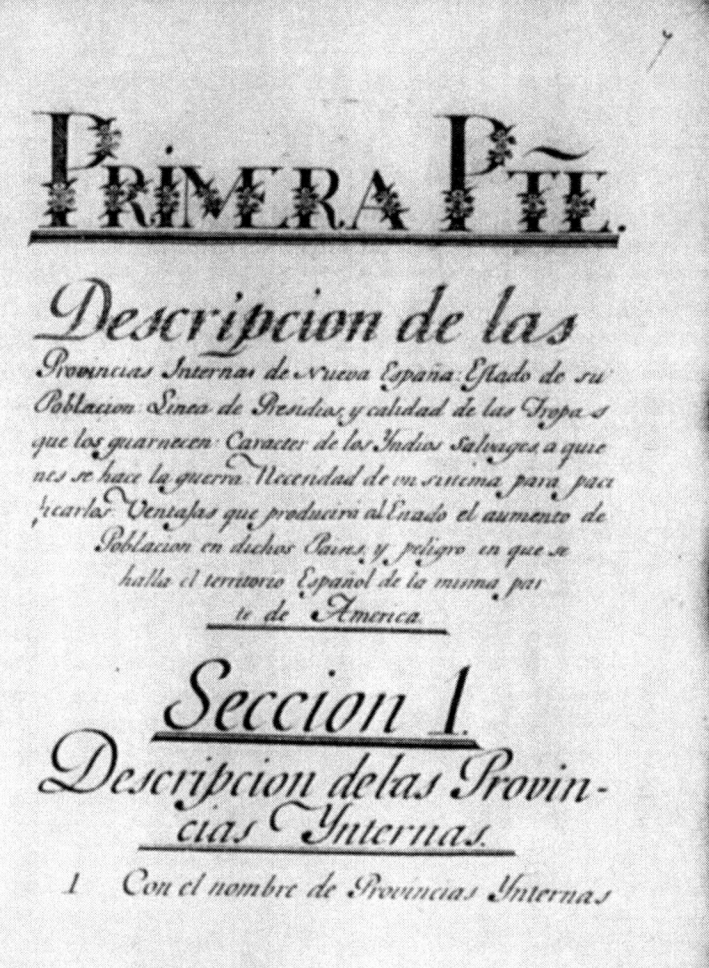

Folio 6, Cortés *Memorias*, Add. Ms. 17652. (Reproduced by permission of the British Library.)

# FIRST PART

*Description of the Interior Provinces of New Spain: the
State of Its Population, the Line of Presidios, and Quality
of the Troops That Garrison Them; Nature of the Savage
Indians Against Whom We Wage War, the Need for a
System of Pacifying Them, the Advantages That Popula-
tion Growth in Said Countries Would Bring to the State,
and the Dangers Facing the Spanish Territories in that
Same Part of America*

## SECTION 1
### Description of the Interior Provinces

1. Known by the name of Interior Provinces are the Californias,
Sonora, Nueva Vizcaya, Nuevo México, Coahuila, Texas, Nuevo
Santander, and Nuevo León. These latter two provinces have been
incorporated into the jurisdiction of the viceroyalty of Mexico. The
colony of the Californias, also subject to that government, is divided
under the names Alta and Baja and receives all its aid and supplies
through the port of San Blas on the Mar del Sur.[3] The Interior Provinces have been elevated recently to a captaincy-general and to a
dependency of the court. Of Nueva Vizcaya, Sonora, Nuevo México, Coahuila, and Texas, I will speak with the greatest method and
order possible within the limitations I have imposed upon myself.

2. The five aforementioned provinces are situated between 22°
55' and 38° north latitude, with several other lands occupying the
territory included between these two parallels, and their extremes
from west to east are situated between 260° 57' and 284° 49' east
longitude from Tenerife.[4] Their climate is benign, except for various
sites on the coasts. The four seasons of the year make themselves
felt with the fullest impact, especially the winter and summer. In the
former one experiences cold, snow, and ice, and in the latter the

21

heat reaches comparable extremes, tempered by the rains that are so frequent in that season. Finally, the climate is salubrious, and epidemics are rarely, if ever, seen. The sky is serene, and the land is an impressive spectacle.

3. One appreciates in the vast expanse of these countries the three realms of Nature. There is a fertile soil which, with little manual effort, yields every grain and fruit in abundance. The natural pastures and meadows are covered with grass, and the hillsides and banks of rivers and streams abound with thick, robust trees. The province of Sonora contains very admirable woods, some for luxury furniture and others for use in dyes. The province of Texas could furnish many lumberyards with timber for construction. This rich portion of America is irrigated by abundant rivers and an infinite number of streams. In the former breed various kinds of fish, and the latter bestow their water to the surrounding soil.

4. No exaggeration can convey the aptness of these provinces for the raising and maintaining of all kinds of livestock. It can be shown that without the livestock exported from these provinces to the viceroyalty of Mexico, neither its inhabitants nor its great mining operations could subsist. And if one were to add up all the thefts and damages this industry has suffered from the Indians during their cruelest hostilities, it would seem amazing that they had not finished off the very last ones and that the herds survive. But what better proof could be offered than to observe in some of the northern frontier lands numerous herds of wild horses, vast and lovely plains covered with buffalo, and an extreme abundance of every kind of game, large and small, which sustain so many Indian nations? Neither is there a scarcity of the winged species, and one can see birds unknown either in Europe or in the hot climes of America.

5. The mineral realm is a fertile enough field to fill volumes. The Royal Mint in Mexico can provide reports full of data on the treasures that have come, and still come, from Nueva Vizcaya in bars of silver. Sonora is one of the most precious provinces in America, having provided much silver and gold. In proof of the abundance of the latter metal, it is enough to recall the Real de la Cieneguilla placer mine and many others.[5] The riverbeds carry grains of gold that maintain many Indians and increase the prosperity of traders. The best experts affirm that there is no piece of land which does not contain a greater or lesser quantity of grains or par-

ticles of gold. The most convincing proof of the abundance of silver and gold in the two aforesaid provinces of [Nueva] Vizcaya and Sonora are the many bars, disks, and grains that are offered in trade with the royal account by private individuals, as well as the shipments that mine owners forward to the aforesaid Royal Mint. In such a vast domain there are but few hacienda owners who have the necessary draft animals and fields. The rest are poor and barely established, content to scratch their meager subsistence from the soil, lacking the knowledge and resources necessary to undertake the enterprises that would make them prosperous. Finally, there are mines operating in Coahuila, as well as in Texas and New Mexico, but the nascent population of these latter two provinces is far too sparse for the many objectives of industry and other opportunities that arise. In New Mexico we know of copper mines of rare purity, where not even a fifth of the ore is lost as dross.[6] There are especially noteworthy gypsum mines. There the stones are extracted in the form of tablets and washed in boiling water, leaving marks for inserting a blade for the purpose of cutting slices the thickness of a *línea*.[7] They emerge as diaphanous as glass, and so they are used for the comfort of dwellings in that remote province. There are also sulphur, jet, and other types of mines, and it is evident that throughout the Interior Provinces there are rare commodities that would greatly enrich this realm of natural history.

6. The two seas that serve as the eastern and western limits of the aforesaid provinces are the Gulf of Mexico and the Gulf of California. Coastal navigation of the former requires experience, but up to now it has been more feared than explored. Because of this failing we know only that there are abundant fish along the coast, succoring those who have navigated it and sustaining the Indians who inhabit the neighboring islands. The Gulf of California has been, and continues to be, frequented by smaller ships of the king, and the mail crosses it to Loreto in order to maintain communications with the Californias. On its eastern margin, along the coast of Sonora, and even in the Yaqui River there is pearl fishing, which with more concentrated effort would bring abundant harvests. They have extracted very large pearls of a beauty and color comparable to those of the Orient.

7. To conclude with a brief overview of these two seas, it must be pointed out, with regard to the Gulf of Mexico, that the string of

islands flanking its coast was unknown. Nor was it known that brigantines and other ships of equal size could cross the bar of the Río Grande del Norte without the slightest danger. There was no information about the port of Galveston, and information about the Bay of San Bernardo, or Espíritu Santo,[8] was very inaccurate. The port of Galveston is good, clean, and sheltered. Its bar has a depth of 18 to 21 feet and its interior measures 5 or 6 fathoms. The bar at the Bay of San Bernardo has a depth of 9 to 12 feet and its interior measures 4 to 5 fathoms up to a distance of 4 miles. The rest is a spacious lagoon that extends to the mouth of the Colorado de las Cañas,[9] Guadalupe, and San Antonio rivers. On the coast of Sonora we only hear of the bay of Mazatlán,[10] but the bay of Guaymas is more valuable, it being a commodious, clean, and very secure harbor. And there are other well-sheltered landings that would be of great service if the coast were settled along its entire length.

# SECTION 2
## Report on the Population and on the Practical Arts

1. The population of these five provinces is very sparse, numbering no more than three hundred thousand inhabitants. It is distributed among two insignificant cities, several *villas*[11] that exist in name only, mining settlements, small villages, and haciendas and ranchos, with a very small percentage gathered under the protection of the presidios.

2. Agriculture makes no progress, nor can it do so in provinces so vast and sparsely populated, whose settlements are separated by awesome lonely wastes. It is limited to local consumption. Cattle raising constitutes the wealth and property that provides a meager income for hacienda owners. While cattle are consumed in the territory, the majority are exported to the provinces nearest to Mexico City. Manufacturing and crafts are unknown; from Mexico City, Puebla de los Angeles, and the province of Michoacán they bring back supplies of cheap cloth, manufactures of the same class, and other items of a similar nature.

# SECTION 3
## The Line of Presidios and the Quality of the Troops That Garrison Them

1. The military force of such an extended territory consists of twenty presidial companies, five flying companies, two companies of Opata Indians, and one of Pima Indians, whose total strength amounts to 3,099.

2. The true frontier line should be understood to consist of the following presidios: Tucson, Buenavista, Santa Cruz, Bavispe, and Fronteras in Sonora; Janos, San Buenaventura, Carrizal, and San Eleazario in Nueva Vizcaya; Babia or Santa Rosa, Monclova, Aguaverde, and Rio Grande in Coahuila; and Béxar and Bahía del Espíritu Santo in Texas. The presidial company of Santa Fe should be considered an advanced post beyond the line whose purpose is to defend as well as possible the province of Nuevo México, which is situated above all the other posts that form the aforementioned frontier. The other presidial companies occupy, within the domain of our territory, positions that have been deemed advantageous, and the same is true of the five flying companies and that of the Opata Indians of Bacuachi.

3. The king's troops defending this territory deserve much praise. They are faithful, long-suffering, and of such humble character that the most reverent obedience comes to them by nature. Exposure to the elements for fifty days or more does not bother them. They live on horseback day and night and travel with such determination that it is amazing to see the territory they can traverse in a very short time. They enter combat with courage and tenacity, and this circumstance varies only when their officers and corporals fail to set them an example. The most amazing thing is the frugality with which they sustain themselves: a bit of toasted corn flour dissolved in water is their main nourishment,[12] and on rare occasions some biscuit or cracker and a very small portion of the supplies of sugar loaves that they call sweets. Supplied with these provisions, they can undertake any mission, even though it may be over a great distance and time, as long as they are confident that once the expedition is concluded they will be returning to their homes. As

regards what should be their most effective training, I will venture to say that it is inconsistent. Given exercises that are never of any use to them, they recognize this and look upon the exercises with some disdain. The soldier of the Interior Provinces must be a capable marksman and perfect with the musket on foot or on horseback. This is the expertise they most need, yet it is not the one given the most attention. With the assurance that their shots would hit their mark at a medium distance and at a quick aim, they would be formidable and defy the arrows, and the Indians, even in situations where they were in great numbers, would be the victims of their resistance. This argument is based on an infallible principle: the arrow is so swift and penetrating that nothing can stop it when it is fired at close range. But past that range its aim begins to falter, and if it then hits a target it either inflicts a slight wound or falls away because its flight is spent. Thus, if the soldier is a good marksman, he can make a sure kill of his adversary when it is possible. He will look with disdain on the Indians' capacity to loose many arrows before he can load and shoot his musket. Thus would we avoid the heavy spilling of blood that ordinarily occurs in most attacks. It so happens that, even when they are very close to one another, our soldiers do not manage enough offense in relation to the number of shots they fire.

4. In all justice, the two companies of Opatas are also deserving of honorable praise. There are no words to express exactly the consideration merited by these strange Indian soldiers, who are worthy of all the government's esteem for their outstanding qualities. And we should recognize their exemplary loyalty since the time of their subjugation, as if they were the Tlaxcalans[13] of northern New Spain. They gladly volunteer to fill any vacancy that occurs in either of their two companies, and they accept the post with as much gratitude as if they had received an appointment of honor and trust. They elect their officers from among themselves, at the same pay as that of a private. They are totally subordinate to a subaltern Spanish officer, who is the company commander, and to the Spanish sergeant or sergeants assigned to them. They head off on campaign with incredible ardor. They can travel twenty or thirty leagues on foot in a day, at the same pace at which each of the other troops would have worn out two or three mounts. What is more, when the battle is joined no deer can match their quickness and agility in leap-

ing from rock to rock and reaching the highest peaks of the mountains. The Apaches, who have been raised in the mountains and have learned all the defensive points and escapes, acknowledge the superiority of the Opatas. To characterize one's extreme agility, they say it is as great as that of a Concho, which is what they call them.[14] This soldier begins the attack with either his rifle or his bow, both of which weapons he uses. Battle—though they are not by nature violent—is to win or die. When their ammunition has run out, or no arrows remain in their quivers, then their lances and personal aggressiveness determine their fate. They harbor an implacable hatred for all Apaches and all kinds of Indians who are our enemies. Their animosity is such that they cannot be entrusted with prisoners, who fall victim to their hatred. They excuse such horrendous conduct with the unverifiable pretext that the prisoners were conspiring to escape. Such is the character of the Opata soldiers, and it is no exaggeration to say that the other troops would have had few victorious encounters without their help. They deserve greater esteem, and their pay should be equal to that of soldiers in a presidial or flying company. They are quite valuable to the royal service, yet in recent years they have been removed from the posts where they have their companies and families and taken to fight in the provinces of Vizcaya and Coahuila, without returning to their homes in one or even two years.

5. We must also increase these troops as much as possible and foster their families in the towns of Bavispe, Bacuachi, and others in their native territory, so that the number of such loyal Indians might grow. The last *visita*, or review, made of this nation showed that it consisted of a thousand men capable of bearing arms, and that the entire nation recognizes and obeys an Opata chief, so designated for his good qualities by the commandant general of the Interior Provinces and granted the title of general of the nation.

6. The company of Pima Indians, located at San Rafael de Buenavista, has soldiers of a different complexion. They set out in search of the enemy and attack him with all the fire and fury of good warriors. But if resistance is strong, and if they see that any of their own are killed or injured, they lose heart, disperse, and retreat in total disorder.

# SECTION 4
## Indians with Whom We Are at War

1. The nations against which we fight at present are known by the name of Apaches, courageous Indians whose character I will discuss later. It has been and continues to be our absurd and foolish belief that they are impossible to force into peace and the customs of a rational life, but this is a most patent fallacy. They love peace and hate to lose it. Since the year 1786,[15] when we began to fight them with greater expertise and tactics, we have seen many *rancherías* from different tribes come in to seek peace. It is true that some *rancherías* have struck their encampments and gone to seek refuge in their mountains, but if we examine their reasons in honest truth, we will find that they are justifiable. It is no inconstancy to break the peace when agreements have been breached, for everyone knows that such conduct is employed by the most civilized powers boasting the highest human character, and with whose grievances the entire world can sympathize and find justification.

2. He who has knowledge of the life and constitution of the savage Indians of northern New Spain must establish the basic principle that, in order to bring them out of the mountains and keep them in settlements, it is vital to provide them aid to cover their major needs. It is also clear that they have no other means of providing for themselves than hunting and stealing. Thus, if they are deprived of these two methods, especially the latter, they will perish and will be forced to return to the nomadic life which they led and which, with all its risks, allows them to survive. As mentioned above, numerous Indian groups have descended from the mountains in peace, and we have agreed to give them a ration of meat and corn, some tobacco, and from time to time some tool or medicine that they might lack. These expenses, if seen with measured reason, are quite moderate and of great service to the King, the State, and the inhabitants of the Interior Provinces, because the robberies the Indians can commit in one week and the blood they spill in their raids are more costly than any amount they could consume.

3. The conditions agreed to when they came to seek peace have not been fulfilled, and their ration has dwindled in violation of a pact that should have been observed solemnly as an example to instill in

them the proper notion of the honor and rectitude of the Spanish. Despite all this and our having caused them indirectly to have to abandon our embrace, very few of them have followed that course, and the majority have accepted the alterations and the repeated reductions that have occurred. We have seen at the same time that other *rancherías* with no rations or aid whatsoever are content to make treaties so that we will not harm them, and they will live in peace and calm without attacking us. Under these conditions they locate wherever they are commanded and give constant proof of their good faith. Is this to be uncontrollable? Could one find a more rational disposition among any savage nations, who cannot always observe in us those moral virtues that might reward them? By any chance is it impossible to settle the friendly Indians who live at our presidios and who, when they need to go hunting to provide food and clothing for their families, humbly ask the commanding officer of the post for a temporary written permit indicating their destination, and who, whenever they see a party of troops, no matter how small, approach and present their permit, which they carefully preserve as a safeguard for their lives? The barbarous Indians submit to this conduct, but that is nothing in comparison to other examples of greater importance.

4. Consider the case where a party sets out on campaign and its commanding officer asks for four, six, or more *indios de paz*[16] as auxiliaries, well aware that without them he would accomplish little or nothing. The word goes out to the selected *ranchería* and all the men capable of bearing arms come in so that the most reliable might be chosen. The rest, left in shame and sadness because they were not allowed to go along, beg, redouble their pleas, and are seized with the greatest sorrow when it all has proven fruitless. I have witnessed this in person on several occasions. Some of them return to where their *rancherías* are located to care for their families and the families of the others, while the other chosen ones go about happy and proud for having achieved our trust. And what do these Indians do? From the time that they leave our frontier, or the limits of controlled territory, they guide the troops through country which the latter do not know, they conceal them so they will not be detected, and they halt where there is grass and good watering places. Two or three of the Indians tell the detachment commander to wait while they go to observe and determine the situation of the *rancherías* of

the Indians they intend to attack. They return within the short time they promised and almost totally lead the attack in this insidious warfare, which is the most common way of operating and is very rarely otherwise. They surprise those considered to be enemies, and the Indian auxiliaries are the first to fight as lions. And against whom? Against their kin, against their countrymen, and against men for whom, given their similarity of customs and way of life, they should feel more affinity than to us. Finally, they die in combat with the greatest loyalty and gallantry. These facts are well known and corroborated by everyone from the lowest private to the commander of the party. It is to be believed that the soldiers would exaggerate nothing that might detract from the glory of their own good success. If these operations do not give a precise idea that these Indians are resources that we must cultivate, then I do not know what we should wait for in order to look upon them with sure expectations and to adopt wiser policies toward them. Poor Indians! Let us pity them for a moment. It is true that they have often exercised the natural inconstancy that is attributed to them, and that they have committed excesses common to men already held to be our enemies. But if the Indians had a defender who could represent their rights on the basis of natural law, an impartial judge could soon see that every charge we might make against them would be offset by as many crimes committed by our side. There are old and recent documents that cover and support my assertion.

# SECTION 5
## The Need to Pacify the Apache Nations

1. To attract and settle the Apache Indians is the most important goal facing us in the Interior Provinces of New Spain. All the interests of a wise policy rest on this point, as do those of humanity and religion. This is the business that calls most for a sane, deliberate, and thought-out system that will reduce to basic principles the pacification and permanent stabilization of the Indians in our territories. Without it the Interior Provinces will never know happiness and, while the horror of their raids might cease, it will only be for a while. They will renew them with deadly strikes as bloody and atrocious as before. Our possession of the country in that sense is in no way absolute; we possess it in such a way that we

only manage to keep troubles far away from the provinces that are considered to be civilized and are free of such neighbors.

2. Let us receive as many Indians as seek peace, whether attracted by gentle persuasion or forced by the repeated campaigns, pursuit, and destruction that we wreak on them in their mountains. Let us negotiate with them clearly and distinctly everything to be granted to them, and let that agreement be given the most prompt and constant fulfillment. Let us express our esteem to them, yet punish their excesses with an air of severity and justice, determining the corrections and punishments in proportion to the crimes which they commit. These points must not be lost from view in the admission of *indios de paz*. There must not be the slightest variability among them, and they must be closely watched. Thus may we guarantee the permanent pacification and tranquility of the Indians. When it has gone on for twelve or fifteen years, this peaceful life will be very pleasant for them, whereas the savage and beleaguered existence which they lead in the mountains will seem quite violent. One would never accomplish anything by forcing them to engage in agriculture. While a few have a fair aptitude for this natural industry, those who do not seek this type of occupation should not be forced. Their first generation[17] would be the effective one upon which all our attention should focus, to make them understand that work will allow them to live in comfort. It is right to provide all the proper aid to these and to those of the former who seek it. This is a sure and timely conquest, and the grandchildren of the savage, fierce, destructive, and bloody Indians would become useful subjects, as humble and religious as the other peoples that the Spanish monarch has ruled on the American continent since his subjects began its conquest.

3. This vital subject is now reduced to a precise concept so that we may base on a central maxim the pacification of the Indian nations known by the generic name of Apaches. This should create a rather long-term system for the administration and control of this delicate program, without losing sight of local customs, the nature of the Indians, and the current administration of the presidios, in short, of certain efforts which will mutually check one another and preserve order. But to explain this, or elaborate the thought, would stray from the course of the brief indication I have determined to write.

## SECTION 6
## The Increase of the Population is the First Consideration,
## and It Is Highly Important That Experienced Governors
## Be Appointed
## to Rule Overseas Territories

1. None of the institutions called for by politics, none of the brilliant programs which military science can engender, and none of the improvements prescribed by public order for the welfare of the people, can be fulfilled or achieve their ends if the spirit guiding their execution, or the man in command, wavers or veers from the path. With such a clear axiom firmly in my imagination, I can affirm that not only is it important that new regulations or programs be entrusted exclusively to individuals of rectitude and solid obedience, but also that they have proven skills with which to carry to fulfillment the specific developments which each matter presents, according to the unexpected events, disturbances, or vicissitudes to which human affairs are subject. All the world's peoples are content when they are governed by such men. Then, even those troubles that come from divine providence are mitigated to the extent possible.

2. On this foundation I base my argument, that even when the devoted Ministry of our Spain applies some measure toward the important goal of promoting the progress of which the Interior Provinces are naturally capable, we must not forget to propose to the king officers of great probity and recognized skill to whom to entrust his command. I express this sentiment because that sure selection is of the greatest importance in such countries, that is to say, in every region where things are very much at a beginning, and some entirely primitive. If we do not choose able commanders who are disinterested and free of other concerns, all attempts at improvement will be in vain. Permit me to recall here the obvious results of the good government enjoyed in the past and present by several provinces or districts of the Indies when they have been blessed

with good leaders: men who have been examples of disinterest, virtue, and moderation. But we will also make the painful recollection of others who have come with an insatiable thirst for wealth, their hearts possessed of the most harmful and devouring greed. To this plague, already too common among those who go to work in the Indies, accrue even worse circumstances: the fierce and horrendous problem of despotism. With it officials become insufferable and treat the king's subjects as their slaves. Such treatment is not deserved by such humble and submissive subjects, who not only accept and acknowledge all distinctions of a person's class or hierarchy, but kneel to them and obey their orders with unquestioned veneration. Thus, the inhabitants and natives of America behave and will behave with humility and great love for their sovereign. But the officials to whom such abuses are habitual are unworthy of the command and authority delegated to them. The people suffer them as the heaviest yoke, speaking only of the day when they will be replaced. As long as memory endures they are detested.

3. This is one of the main sources of themes for foreign writers,[18] who, under the cover of the facts of such abominable behavior, heap their poisonous and noxious sort of envy, seeking in such a base manner to conceal the treachery and bad faith with which their fellow countrymen have taken over territories in both the Indies. They plunge ahead without shame and with no more basis than the above (of which the supreme government could not be aware), to the ridiculous extreme of obscuring the brilliant and glorious conquests of the Spanish. They know the weakness of their arms and do not hesitate to resort to the iniquitous games of deceit and claims which feed their viperous tongues. They only reap the scorn and contempt of intelligent and impartial readers, while the high reputation of our heroes of notable and immortal memory remains steadfast. Not even the privileges of conquerors nor their distances from the metropolis swayed them from the spirit of justice or from their desire to establish their religion—two of the principles most consonant with the beneficent aims of our sovereigns, who, looking from the outset upon the inhabitants of the conquered overseas territories as natural subjects, have issued very charitable, improved, and reformed laws over time as experience has required.[19]

4. To focus on the central matter of this section, I state that we have discussed the vital necessity of pacifying the Apache Indians as

the means of achieving the public good and subsistence of the Interior Provinces. This aim brings with it the growth of the population, the most essential aspect of reaching all our goals. When the Indians are settled, they and their families will contribute to this growth, and when the natives are free from the scourge of hostilities there will be an end to the horrendous spilling of blood which they have caused, the number of whose victims, as could be listed here, would inspire the greatest sorrow. Ultimately, the citizens would prosper, and all sectors would experience a phenomenal increase. This security and the elimination of danger would attract new colonists. Overland commerce would also take on a movement and ferment very unlike the languid and passive state it is in today. Consumption would increase and exports would be considerable.

5. Population is the central point where all plans must be rooted. It will be a great fountain of wealth, and that population itself will constitute the strongest bulwark to defend the territory. What population there is today, and what could be, must be promoted by overcoming obstacles: for its welfare, peace must be achieved; to defend and preserve it, vigorous war must be waged when there is no other choice; and to relieve it, all the aid and supplies which the troops can provide must be sent. The benefits of this are even greater for the King and State than for the very subjects directly receiving the aid.

# SECTION 7

## Regarding the European Nation
## That Can Most Easily Invade the Spanish Colonies
## from the Part of America under Discussion

1. Dangers of grave importance and of difficult remedy threaten our territories in the northernmost part of America. We must be quite vigilant in its northwestern part and along the Misoury River. The nation that encroaches upon us at the aforesaid points and the one that advances upon us from the other side will not be satisfied: the first [Great Britain], with having provided clear proof of its ambitions, and the other [the United States], with the enlargement of its new boundaries and the population growth which it has achieved.

2. Once the ambitious designs of the first nation are realized, while the second proceeds to the point necessary to make its power more respectable and even fearsome, the empire of New Spain will fall into such disarray that its possessions cannot even term themselves having a shared dominion, although the spirit of conquest, which opens the way to other easy enterprises, may subside. The royal budget might not be enough for state officials, and the exclusive trade with the Spanish nation would be so weak that, without another drastic expulsion, every individual would be forced to direct their efforts along other paths. I am going to state what I feel and what I understand, and I ask with the utmost humility that I be forgiven for the errors which I may commit on such a delicate theme. I admit my lack of education and that I have no skills to discuss it. I only hope that I will be pardoned, because of my deep love of the King, for this work which I consecrate to the Fatherland, and for my desire that it be covered in glory, a perpetual glory capable of imposing respect and of triumphing over its enemies.

3. This same sincerity which shields me does not allow me to speak on this matter with ambiguity and facile judgments regarding the European nation whose proximity and establishment on the northwestern shores of America we must watch most closely. We must fear and watch the English nation, striving to the utmost to destroy its determined notions and any expeditions that it might attempt in that area.

4. The English know perfectly well what their interests are and they know ours as well. We must become familiar with theirs, and we will find that, whether friends of good or bad faith, and enemies either covert or in open war, our commercial relations are always intimately linked with theirs. From this it follows that their maxims and their spirit of self-interest will seek to dispossess us at all times and in every place where the Spanish banner waves. We must repel by equal means that constant element aimed at our destruction. The reciprocal contrast in our rivalries must necessarily bring discord, and with it the motives for a break, which will be as frequent as allowed by the state of strength in which each nation finds itself and by the alliances which each one may form. The theater of our war with them must always be America and the Philippine Islands. Our fortune will be subject to other causes, which will be at the center of a favorable or adverse result.

5. The English nation, without deprecation of the merit and good name which make it worthy of esteem, is well known for its limitless ambition, for the extreme which its pride has reached, and for its immediate passion for destroying all foreign commerce. It seeks to be the absolute master of it, to enchain the known world with its empire, and through the riches and the preponderance of this system—so dear to the heart of the King of Great Britain, the Ministry, and the entire nation—to oppress and subjugate the other nations, becoming the Queen of the Sea with the considerable strength and ascendancy that naturally would derive from its control. It is important to oppose the ideas regarding us that the English have already made known many times, but also to cut short these reflections, which might senselessly distract me from the point for which I have discussed them. I will now proceed to deal with the main question, by saying that the English are anxious to establish themselves in the aforementioned part of the American continent, that they have the means to do so, that it will be very detrimental to us, and that all of our efforts to dislodge them would be quite fruitless once they are established and fortified.

6. Since English power began to grow in the East Indies, this nation has overlooked no measure that might make possible its establishment in the part of the Americas that has been indicated, despite the memorable treaty that prohibits it. The fur trade, the new advantages which it might achieve with those Indians, and the expectation of the smuggling which its proximity would allow it to carry on along our coasts are surely their intents, constituting a second level of trade. To achieve this, its vigilance has omitted no effort that might bring about its intent. A few years ago, what voyages and new discoveries fanned their hopes! But they would have preferred more than these attempts to extend their possessions north of the Río de San Lorenzo,[20] which would have opened their way to the Pacific Ocean. The one that Mr. Hearn[21] made in 1772 left no doubt that by that route it was not possible to achieve their aim, nor was it in their interest to reach the sea at the latitude to which said explorer ascended. They would only have managed to make another contribution to the advances that geography has made in those regions so little known up to now. Then they had another hope: that the vast extension that lay between the Pacific Ocean, Lago Ounopique,[22] and Lago Pike[23] was a sea that connected with

the former. But the recent exploration by Mr. M'Kensie—departing from Montreal, half the distance along the major part of the San Lorenzo between Quebec and the entrance to Lago Ontario and advancing at between 45 and 50° latitude until emerging at a site on the coast between Nooka Sound and King George's Island—produced new disappointment.[24] Such a laudable enterprise only managed to resolve various points which were matters of disputes and opinions. The hope of finding a passage to said ocean by a more northerly route still persists, but it can be thought that this discovery may not be made or that it might be after one of those great upheavals of the globe which occur once in a great while.

7. We have also learned of the planned expedition to settle and claim Nooka and Fuka, and that our scant naval forces posted there under the command of First Pilot and Frigate Lt. Don Esteban Martínez seized the commission's ships, after treating them carefully, taking possession of the documents that authorized it as well as the appointment papers of the governor for that new colony.[25] This incident caused much indignation in the English government and not a little discord between it and our own. Without a doubt it was the main reason that obliged Spain to quickly equip the fleet that took to sea in the year 1790. Things assumed a new aspect because of the important developments in Europe which were beginning at that time in full force and it was rightly foreseen that they would undergo greater fermentation. It is affirmed that the Spanish government agreed that the English could pursue the fur trade along that coast without establishing posts. There followed immediately the special treaty of alliance between both nations, which from the outset was violated and finally dissolved with the peace with France in the year 1795 and with the war declared on England in the following year of 1796.

8. There cannot remain the slightest doubt that the English will establish and fortify themselves at Nooka and Fuka, and if they have not done so already it is because greater undertakings and larger interests oblige them to transfer and concentrate their attention on Europe. Either with the possession of these two important posts or without it, Alta California is vulnerable to invasion and conquest by a very small force. This territory is quite beautiful and very fertile, with a climate and skies seen nowhere else in America. Its native Indians are numerous and of such good nature and character that they

are the most peaceful known among that caste. Its seas are the most abundant in fish, its harbors famous, and the entire coast so uncluttered and deep that ships of the line can drop anchor very close to it.

9. In order to shorten the summary of this rapid description in accord with my proposed aim, we shall say that that vast country is defended by 223 men, which is the total strength of its four permanent companies, of which a large portion is assigned to protect the missions. Lately the government, not forgetting the attention it must give to such an important colony, has assigned an infantry company called the Catalonian Volunteers and eighteen artillery men. Those reinforcements, with three weak batteries, are supposed to cover that country, but it is not so; California remains as defenseless as before. And that total, which barely comes to three hundred men, divided into four or five parts and posted at intervals of fifty or sixty leagues, is a negligible defense and doubtless will surrender its arms wherever the enemy might appear.

10. We must believe that Monterrey and the remarkable Bay of San Francisco, surrounded by the most fruitful and luxuriant lands and with natural advantages for fortification, would be the points for attack. Were they assaulted simultaneously, Alta California would surely be conquered by merely arriving and taking it. Possessing it, the invaders would descend to Baja California, defended only by the company of forty-seven men stationed at the port of Loreto. This area, which they also call Vieja California, is not so fertile as Nueva California and is more arid. But along its coasts the English would reap great riches from pearl fishing, and they would find themselves in the best situation to introduce contraband along the coast of Sonora and Nueva Galicia. This attack would do considerable damage to commerce in New Spain, and they would take our silver and gold from us in coin and bullion. Let us see what resources there are to reconquer our colony after suffering its loss, setbacks to the royal accounts, and the annihilation of our commerce.

11. A plan for an expedition to cross the Colorado River of the Californias for the purpose of attacking the points held by the enemy would be a reprehensible absurdity, because even if troops were gathered at the most advanced outpost in Sonora, there would still be an enormous distance, capable of tiring and exhausting the most hardened troops. The aforesaid Río Colorado is deep and fordable from its eastern bank in only two or three places at the

height of the dry season. On the west bank there are many populous Indian groups, some of which we do not know well, and others which have proved to us on several occasions to be warlike. Even when we leave these behind, we would continue to encounter others about whose character we have little information, so that, before we ever saw the enemy whom we went to attack, we would encounter many others no less fearsome. And our tasks would multiply, with new fears and problems. Finally, the division might arrive at the post or site chosen for the attack, but fatigue, hunger, and the lack of provisions – with no hope of obtaining them from anywhere – could sap the morale of the troops. With such undeniable consequences, and faced with the necessity of waging a type of warfare to which it was not accustomed, it would be logical to fear that the fruits of such an imprudent policy would be to suffer the misfortune of a total defeat, or, with better preparation, to opt for a dishonorable retreat.

12. It seems that we should consider just coordinating an expedition to set out from two places, so that the attack would be made simultaneously from two sides. The viceroy of New Spain would send to the port of San Blas as many troops as could be carried by the ships that remained, after assigning a select number out of the total fleet to the Gulf of California so that, on the coast of Sonora, the commander general of the Interior Provinces might launch a select division from among the companies that garrison the district under his command. The latter should not set out until it received word that the force from San Blas had reconnoitered the Cabo de San Lucas. In this way, the first force having made its plans to land at Monterrey, and the other at or near Loreto, they might attack the enemy from the front and the rear until the vigor of their assault forced it to unconditional surrender. The execution of this plan is subject to other partial concerns which are well known to officers trained in the art of war and to those experienced in it, who know how to lead their troops, pushing or halting their marches, and keeping in mind that all elements must work as a single body and that none of them is to act independently of it, unless it is with the assurance of achieving victory with greater probability than the total force. This is one of the missions that we could undertake with the greatest certainty of a successful outcome, but pure and simple reflection shows that it would still run the risk of failure.

13. This expedition would be more or less vigorously organized, according to the attitudes, the ideas, or suggestions of the persons with whom the two commanders consult. A favorable outcome could also be threatened by the leadership and the decisions of the officers commanding the division, who might not be chosen with the most essential qualities of courage, training, and judgment. Another obstacle immediately arises, and that is the poor quality of the troops of infantry and dragoons in the army of New Spain. Without mentioning everything I feel about this matter, it must be stressed that their vices and low morale are more apparent than is the hope that they might fulfill their duties as good soldiers. Those who defend the frontiers of the Interior Provinces are of a very different character and of better quality, but we do not know whether, accustomed as they are to make war in isolated platoons and each for himself, they would be able, opportunely and in those cases where circumstances and actions demand it, to form into battle columns, maintain order and unity in all their maneuvers, keep up a sustained fire, and fill the gaps caused in their ranks by enemy rifles, cannon, and grapeshot from their batteries. What is certain is that their officers would be of little influence upon them in this regard, because most of them are as little trained and ignorant as the simple private.

14. To these misgivings so pertinent to our situation should be added the vigilance of the defenders who, mindful of the importance of maintaining their conquered colonies, would fortify with the greatest care the point, or points, of greatest concern. And in addition to the troops of the line that might garrison the posts, they would not fail to avail themselves of the native Indians through the gifts, deceptions, and persuasions that the English nation knows how to employ when it suits its purpose, even before the immediate step of subjugating them with the cruelest tyranny. They would put weapons in their hands, take advantage of the feeble defense they might make, and, by spilling the blood of those wretches, would preserve their strong forces for more critical situations. Finally, depending upon the disputes that might arise between one government and another, they could easily dispatch some of the warships which they constantly station in India, by which measure they would destroy the brigantines and one or two smaller frigates being prepared at San Blas.

15. Everything that has been considered and stated on this sub-ject is no illusion. I have sought to speak with ordered logic, leaving aside the consequences and secondary arguments in order to con-fine matters precisely to facts and to truth and to what might happen next. What has been discussed regarding the Californias should not be taken as a determined decision, especially if we direct our atten-tion to the banks of the Misoury River. The English are establishing themselves there, and it even seems that they have erected a fort.[26] That location is desolate and empty, surrounded on all sides by ferocious Indians, and offering none of the rich expectations that would motivate them in California. Let us put all this together, now, and construct a reflective analogy. If a company has been formed to trade in furs with the nations of that region, would they not with ever greater drive and determination undertake the conquest which has been discussed?[27] In California they are presented with resources and great expanses that would enrich them, with a plea-sant climate and some settlements where they could attain the com-forts of civilian life.

16. Returning to the significance of this matter with respect to the English settlements on the Misoury—where they have a most prosperous trade in furs, which is the only commodity which the savage Indians trade for the arms, munitions, and medicines they need—it must be said that from that location it is very easy to de-scend to the Interior Provinces of New Spain, especially to New Mexico and Texas. It is a firmly established fact that they have gone to the Indian peoples settled to the north of the latter, offering them firm and constant friendship, cheap trade, and assurances that the English alone will be their good friends, with whom they will escape the tyranny and persecution of the French and Spanish. It was also learned that a force of nine thousand warriors, urged by the same English nation, was gathering at certain points along the Misisipi to invade our possessions.[28] If the plan had been carried out, or if it is undertaken in the future, I foresee with the greatest sorrow that the consequences will be very tragic for us.

# SECTION 8
## Dangers That Threaten the Northern Part of Spanish America with the Proximity of the Anglo-Americans

1. The other nation that demands our vigilant caution, and forces us to contain, in part, its expansion, is the new power known as the Republic of the United Anglo-American Provinces.[29] These states, which have risen so suddenly to such a colossal height, have extended to points so dangerously near and surround us so closely that we must fear the expansion of their borders over Louisiana and Florida and their proximity to the province of Texas, where they can enter undetected. The developments that will emerge in time will bear out my fearful warning, and then the consequences will be more tragic: they will be incurable and permanently damaging, despite the most favorable advantages that we might derive from the changes.

2. We have seen this republic founded in a part of the world where it was not foreseen that any states could be created or consolidated, but rather that the absolute and arbitrary power of the European nations would be the expectation for the country which they might dominate, conquer, acquire, or even enter. We already marvel at a power whose government everyone applauds. It has begun with great fanfare and its progress to date should leave us no doubt as to the heights it can achieve.

3. Once the passions that were so well directed and were part of the overall achievement of the Anglo-North American revolution subsided, and the final hurdle to assure their independence was cleared with the peace of 1783, these men of glorious legacy devoted themselves to the most practical and advantageous ends: that is, to give to their government and their laws a perfection that has been the clarion uniting millions of educated men with arts and sciences; to foment agriculture, of whose product they reap such harvests; to expand their fleets and commerce with a swiftness that surprises us; and to beautify their cities with the most scrupulous order.[30]

4. In history, one finds no example, in a comparable climate of ideas, where a country has increased its population as much as has

the United States of America. In the previous year of 1790 it was no more than 3,929,326 inhabitants, while today it probably exceeds six million.[31] This increase of more than two million souls not only implies in itself the greatness and fortune that so solidly accrue by this means to a region with a climate and soil capable of sustaining and enriching them, but also the infallible certainty that the greater part of this increase has been in educated men who have carried forth with great splendor progress in the sciences, the arts, trade, and even the military profession. This is a treasure that no money can buy, and its effects are as brilliant as its causes are admirable.

5. The breadth and fertility of the land invited them and made it possible to create new districts. There are no longer thirteen Anglo-American states; in a very short time three additional ones have been formed with the same swiftness that their prosperity has grown. KentuKey, near Ylinoa, can, with the greatest dispatch, send fifty thousand vigorous fighting men into war. They could easily advance one hundred or more leagues,[32] entrusting their subsistence solely to the musket or rifle. The state of Cumberland, which occupies lower lands, has been populated with the same swiftness, driving the Indians from their lands, and forcing them to move to the west banks of the Misisipi, thus constituting an indirect step against the tranquility of the Interior Provinces of New Spain. The latest state to be created is Tenisse, or Ternessee, south of the Ohio River.[33] Its population has grown in the same way, and they give their towns a beautiful layout, with all the comforts of life. This is an attraction that silently summons men to society and gives respectability to their settlements. This is the reason why the new city of Washington has emerged so soon after its founding with seven thousand dwellings.

6. It occurred to the Anglo-Americans that without peace with their neighbors to the north, their thoughts should not be distracted by other interests. They decided to make a solemn peace treaty with the Indians of the so-called Six Nations, by which said states abandon and forget their designs on the territories of the Oneyga, Onandago, and Ceyga, and—with this detachment—the rights they wanted to establish in order to acquire the aforesaid territories.[34] On this basis the borders have been drawn, so that all future disputes and disagreements have been anticipated. For their part, the Six Nations renounce all claims regarding the territory settled by the sub-

jects of the United States, and agree to allow them to establish communications between Fort Schuyler and Lake Erie, and permit the Anglo-Americans to frequent all the shores and navigate all the rivers in the lands of the Six Nations. The United States commits itself by these concessions to make immediate payment of a moderate sum of dollars, or pesos, and then of four thousand five hundred dollars each year. Thus, with this treaty the American Republic has achieved not only a lasting peace and considerable advantage in the field of trade involved there, but also a widely recognized demarcation of boundaries, being a line drawn from the head of the mountain range of the Apalaches to the east of Lake Erie, proceeding from there to the northeast to the Hudson River. The Six Nations occupy the region beyond the aforementioned head of the Apalache Mountains, Lake Ontario, and the Hudson. Between the latter and the easternmost part of Ontario is Fort Schuyler.

7. They have also concluded a treaty with Great Britain, signed in London on November 19, 1794.[35] This is one of the most serious reasons obliging the Spanish government to remain alert and pay the most careful attention to the conduct of the Anglo-American Congress. The North American people objected to the agreement and to what was set forth in the aforementioned treaty. They cried that it threatened their political survival and the growth of their commerce, and that it hindered the prosperity of their merchant fleet. Finally the treaty has been ratified by all the states. It can be inferred that the Anglo-American republic will become a close ally of England, and even by itself it is going to become a more considerable power, with a project underway to provide respectable naval forces to protect its trade and free its coasts from all attack and invasion. This last ingredient in their system is precisely the one that will instill some arrogance in the Anglo-American Republic, whose thought up to now we have seen full of moderation. Whatever they undertake will be carried out swiftly. They will not be hindered by a lack of funds; the country is rich and, with their trade, they have more than sufficient resources. Their harvests are so abundant that from the year of 1792 to that of 1794 production grew by twenty-seven million *pesos fuertes*.[36]

8. Even without this proximity, and without the vast territories this nation has acquired through the treaty of San Lorenzo el Real of

October 27, 1795,[37] the United States possessed valuable assets with which to expedite any invasion that it might plan against our provinces. They could marshal their operational force at Fort Pitt, on the banks of the Ohio River, and from that point would only have to descend 250 leagues by waterway to appear at Nachez.[38] There they would need to make all their preparations and safeguards to effect their conquest of Luisiana or the province of Texas by way of Nachitochez.[39] This capability and the expansion that the Anglo-American states have gradually achieved were enough to cause us to live in the greatest apprehension, taking every precaution far in advance, observing their movements, with an astute policy of investigating their every design. It is no longer necessary to extend this observation and precaution over such a distance, and even if we remain on alert with weapons in hand, it would be impossible to avert a surprise. They have extended their borders over thousands of square leagues. They have free navigation of the Misisipi, most of it where we cannot observe them. By the aforementioned treaty all the posts in Ilinoa will be theirs, along with all those on the east bank of the aforesaid river down to 31° north latitude, which appears to include Nachez,[40] the strongest fort in Louisiana. From that point down to the Gulf of Mexico it is only a little over sixty leagues. Let us accept as a demonstrated fact that the Anglo-American plans are very ambitious and there is no doubt that they will be carried out. What misfortune and ruin will not follow after suffering such losses? It is very easy to calculate for those who possess detailed knowledge of those countries, and very demonstrable in view of the documents that provide sufficient information. Natural obstacles emerge at every step of the conquest. The trade monopoly, which provides so much income to our sovereign and enriches the nation, would languish in total inactivity, and most important, who would hold back our enemies henceforth? Would we be free from the ideas and subversive missions that might accompany violence and force? Certainly not. All the great downfalls have a small beginning, and this one is not one of the smallest. I would hope to see in those defenders and officials whom the King has in such important dominions that ardor, that zeal, and that patriotic enthusiasm that make them formidable and crown the fatherland with laurels and glory. Would that their vigorous and brilliant thoughts be suffused with the nerve and wisdom of the

Ministry to repel and severely castigate the enemy in order to quell its ambitious and rapacious spirit. Each of us in particular must rush with ardent loyalty to defend and preserve the integrity of Spanish America, which our ancestors conquered for our beloved sovereigns to the astonishment of the world. Is there a Spaniard who is not honored by the title of nation that distinguishes him when he reads the true history and the heroic deeds that are told in it? If this legacy so honors us and so rightly should make us proud, with what sadness and shame would we not view our past after the greatest and most just Lord had lost a sizable portion of his holdings? In defeat we would say that we still have the name, but not the virtues, nor the love of country, nor the vital spirit. I would also like to eradicate once and for all among many of my compatriots who are known as educated men, the notion that it matters not if we surrender or lose our territories because they are unpopulated, produce nothing, or burden the royal treasury. It matters a great deal, a very great deal. It is a very logical principle not to let one's enemies grow in strength, and all the more so when it is foreseen that such growth can bring our downfall closer, leaving the branches of our possessions as so many dead limbs.

9. It is not with faintheartedness or broken spirit that I warn of so many dangers; all of the threats that have been mentioned are quite apparent, and many more will occur to even the most careless imagination. The soul who speaks here will admit that he has exceeded himself, but his excessive ardor has an honorable and just excuse emanating from his great love for his King and his blind passion for the glory of his fatherland. It is his constant belief that the greatest misfortune and disasters can be diminished when great efforts are centrally combined to fight the oppressors. Unity is a mighty force, and honor is its soul. We must all rouse ourselves with that salutary aim and with this virtue when the sovereign entrusts to us or calls upon us to defend his State. I should consider it my greatest good fortune to be the first soldier on such an occasion, and would to God that the sacrifice of my life, to which my great duty lays claim, were the only victim that might save the Spanish domain from all invasions that might be launched against it.

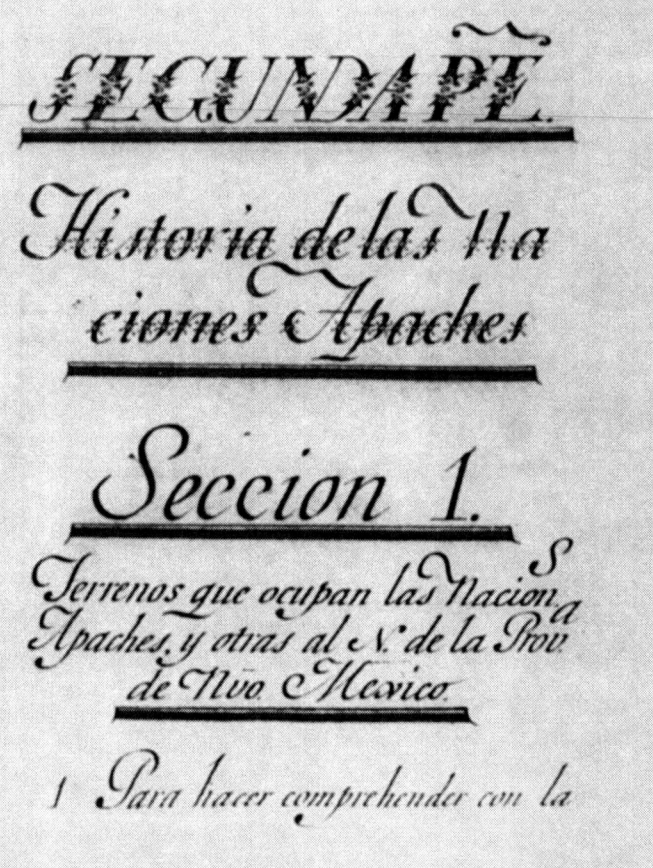

# SEGUNDA PE.

## Historia de las Naciones Apaches

### Seccion 1.

Terrenos que ocupan las Nacion.es
Apaches, y otras al N.° de la Prov.ª
de Nvo. Mexico.

1 Para hacer comprehender con la

Folio 54. Cortés *Memorias*, Add. Ms. 17652. (Reproduced by permission of the British Library.)

# SECOND PART
## HISTORY OF THE APACHE NATIONS

## SECTION 1
### Lands Occupied by the Apache Nations, and Others to the North of the Province of New Mexico[41]

1. To provide as clear an understanding as possible of the nations of savage Indians that inhabit the outer lands of the frontier that forms our boundaries in the Interior Provinces of New Spain, and of the localities they occupy, it is necessary to establish a distinction, creating categories with regard to the nations known by the name of Apaches, others we will introduce called Eastern Nations, those popularly referred to as "Northern," and others called Western Nations. On each point we will offer the clearest information according to the most authentic and truthful reports that have been compiled. And finally we shall omit nothing, in order to give to this fascinating and instructive subject its fullest treatment. We will discuss the nations of savage Indians that inhabit the northern country of the Spanish empire in that part of the world, and in this matter much is to be learned and marveled at.

2. The Spanish know as Apache nations the Tontos, Chiricagüis, Gileños, Mimbreños, Faraones, Mescaleros, Llaneros, Lipanes, and Navajós.[42] All of these tribes are called by the generic name Apaches, and govern themselves independently of one another. There are other nations to which people try to apply the same

Nations of the Internal Provinces, Río Grande to the Pacific. (Map by John V. Cotter.)

name, such as the Xicarillas. Regarding these and the locations occupied by other tribes which are known in the north of New Mexico, we will discuss everything that is known in this second part.

3. The Tontos, also called the Coyoteros, are the westernmost of the Apache nations and the one least known to the Spanish.[43] They are bounded on the west by the nations of the Pápagos, Cocomaricopas, and Yavipais, on the north by the Moguinos,[44] on the south by the Chiricagüis and Gileños, and on the east by the territory between the Mimbreños and Navajós.

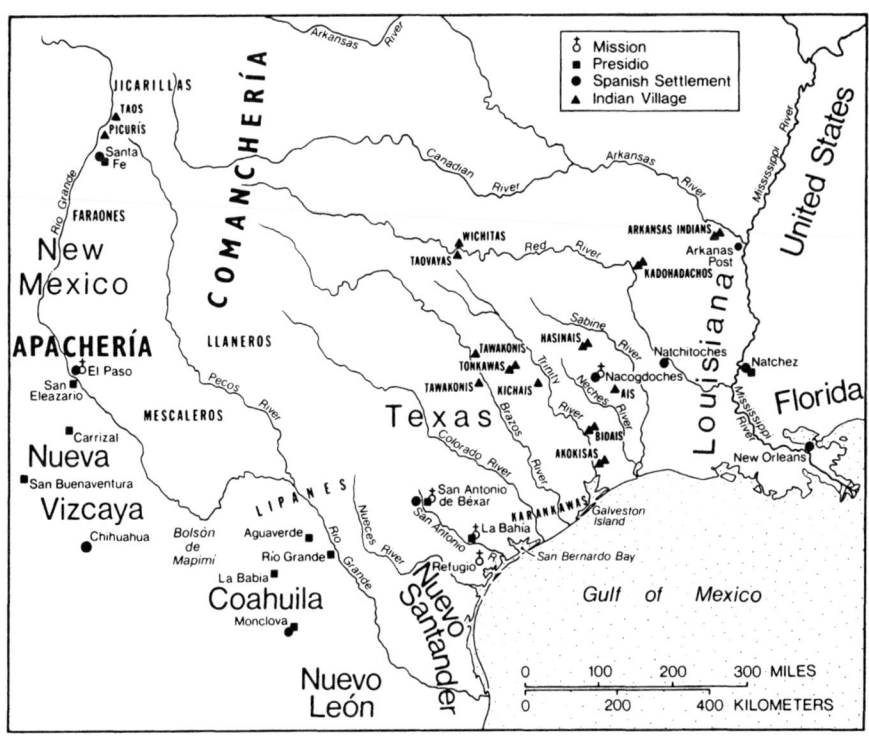

Nations of the Internal Provinces, Río Grande to the Mississippi. (Map by John V. Cotter.)

4. The Chiricagüi nation takes its name from the principal mountain range that it inhabits. It is bounded on the north by the Tontos and Moguinos, on the east by the Gileños, and on the south and west by the Province of Sonora.

5. The Gileños inhabit the mountains adjacent to the Gila River, from which they take their name. They are bounded on the west by the Chiricagüis, on the north by the province of New Mexico, on the east by the Mimbreños, and on the south by our frontier.

6. The Mimbreños, a very large tribe, take their name from the River and Sierras de las Mimbres. They are bounded on the west by the Gileños, on the north by the province of New Mexico, on the

east by the same province, and on the south by part of the frontier of Nueva Vizcaya.

7. The Faraones[45] also constitute a very large group and are believed to be a branch of the Xicarillas. They inhabit the mountains between the Río Grande del Norte and the Pecos. They are bounded on the west by the province of New Mexico, on the north by the same province, on the east by the Mescaleros, and on the south by part of the frontier of Nueva Vizcaya.

8. The Mescalero nation inhabits the mountains adjacent to the Pecos River, on either side, extending south to the mountains that constitute the top of the Bolsón de Mapimí, and ending in that area on the right of the Río Grande. Its terminus on the west is the Faraones tribe, on the north the vast territories of the Cumanchería, on the east the land of the Llanero Indians, and on the south the desert of the Bolsón de Mapimí.[46]

9. The Llanero group is quite numerous, with many warriors. It occupies the great plains and deserts that lie between the Pecos and the left bank of the Río Grande del Norte. This nation is divided into three categories, which are the Natajés, Lipiyanes, and Llaneros. They are bounded on the west by the Mescaleros, on the north by the Cumanches, on the east by the Lipanes, and on the south by our frontier in the province of Cohagüila.

10. The Lipanes form one of the most considerable nations among the savages in northern New Spain. They extend over a vast territory, whose boundaries to the west are the lands of the Llaneros, to the north the Cumanchería, to the east the province of Cohagüila, and to the south the left bank of the Río Grande del Norte, the settlements and presidios of our frontier in Cohagüila being on the right bank.

11. The tribe of Nabajó Indians is the northernmost one of the Apaches. They inhabit the mesas and mountains of the so-called Nabajó Territory, from which they take their name. They do not move their settlements, as do the other Apache nations, and in that country they have built their places or permanent residences, known by such names as Sevolleta, Chicoli, Guadalupe, Cerro-Cavezón, Agua Salada, Cerro-Chato, Chusca, Tumicha, Chellé, and Carriso.[47] All are governed by a captain, whom they respect, and who is now approved by the governor of the province of New Mexico.[48] They are bounded on the west by the Moguinos, on the

north by the Yutas, on the east by the Pueblos of New Mexico, and on the south by the Gileños and Chiricagüis.

12. The Xicarilla Apaches used to inhabit the mountain of the same name in the outlying territories north of the province of New Mexico.[49] The Cumanches drove them from there, and they now live on our borders in the aforesaid province, some of them having come down to the valleys and mountains between the pueblos of Pecuríes[50] and Taos, which are the northernmost of the province.

13. The Yuta nation is very numerous and also consists of various groups, which are distinguishable in name only, and in all else live in perfect peace and harmony. Four of these groups, called the Noaches, Payuchis, Tabiachis, and Sogup, usually occupy lands within the province of New Mexico and generally very close to it on the north and north-northeast. Beyond these, spread over territory for more than two hundred leagues to the north and turning to the northwest, live other Yutas known as Zaguaganas, whose numbers are quite considerable.[51]

# SECTION 2
## Regarding the Apaches' Beliefs, Superstitions, and Marriages[52]

1. The Apache recognize the existence of a Supreme Being and universal Creator with the name of Yastasitan-tan-ne, which is the same as Chief of Heaven. They render him no worship or veneration whatsoever, and, steeped in their ignorance, they totally lack the notions that he might reward the good and punish the evil. Nor do they consider any creature preeminent or a direct servant of the Chief of Heaven. On the contrary, they believe that all are created equally or fashioned by him for his diversion and entertainment, and thus they live in the belief that man's existence lasts until his final annihilation, after a given time which comes to an end through some random misfortune or through the greater or lesser weakness of his nature.

2. This is the principle on which, easily forgetful of the past and tranquilly indifferent toward the future, they devote themselves with the greatest interest and passion to the present, which is where they direct all their aims, without reflection on what happened in times

past or on what might happen in those to come, which is most proper to human endeavors. But in spite of this barbarous and strange system, they attach great importance to entering into agreement and union with some evilly deceitful Indians,[53] upon whom they judge their prosperity and adversity to depend in their current affairs, such assertions giving rise to innumerable delusions.

3. With these ideas, which pass from father to son, they are enthralled in their pernicious judgments, and it is common for them to attribute to some Indian who is an austere and mystic orator the gift for divining. The chosen one enjoys the good faith of his consecrators, accumulating in himself more powers than the others attributed to him. He finds himself held in a regard that distinguishes and benefits him. He plays his role, giving vague responses to those who consult him. On the strength of this practice he becomes more and more convinced of his own powers, while among the others belief is excited in their favored oracle.

4. Allied to this practice is that of medicine, and the application of certain herbs is accompanied by many ceremonies and mournful chants, this being the method that they commonly employ in their healing. But also, when they suffer the misfortune of having one of the Indians of high regard or of the best parentage die in their care, the rumor rises and spreads that the death has been not a natural one, but the result of a spell. Then they seize the diviner, who was so venerated shortly before, and he, in order not to diminish belief in his gift and power, states and confesses that it is true that he cast a spell on the sick man in order to take his life. Then he makes up a lie about how he did it, which never amounts to more than having transferred his saliva to him, corrupting his blood, or some other laughable or absurd means. This declaration is enough for them to tie him to a tree, suspending him just far enough above the ground so that a bonfire that they build beneath him can burn him slowly. Barring these misfortunes, however, their diviners achieve a high degree of respectability, are sought after by distant lands and villages, and are well paid to carry out their two functions explained above.

5. The Apaches are born and reared in the open air of the country, and, fortified by simple foods, are possessed of amazing hardiness. In these nations polygamy is widespread, and each man has as many wives as he can maintain, the number of them being pro-

*Love Songs.* Tempera by Allan Houser. (Courtesy Thomas Gilcrease Institute of American History and Art, Tulsa, Oklahoma.)

*Sneaking Out.* Tempera by Allan Houser. (Courtesy Thomas Gilcrease Institute of American History and Art, Tulsa, Oklahoma.)

portionate to the number of huts or tipis that constitute his settlement.

6. Marriage is performed by the groom buying his intended wife from her father or the relative upon whom she depends.[54] This is the reason for the servile treatment they suffer and why their husbands have control over their very lives. Often a contract will be dissolved by the unanimous consent of the divorcing parties, and the man will return the woman to the father or guardian from whom he obtained her. Other marriages are dissolved by women fleeing from the bad treatment they suffer. In such cases, they take refuge under the protection of one of the most respected men, who takes them in without anyone daring to demand anything of him.

# SECTION 3
## Regarding the Language and Other Particulars of the Natural Character of the Apache Indians

1. The language spoken by all the nations called Apache is one and the same.[55] It varies only in accent and in an occasional regional term, without this difference creating any problem in understanding one another, although the lands where they were born might be very far apart. The pronunciation of this language is quite harsh, but it is not as difficult as first impression might indicate, and once the ear is accustomed, a certain cadence will be found in their words. One realizes that it is lacking in expressions and vocabulary, and this gives rise to an annoying repetition which produces an extremely vague conversation full of gestures. Most notable is the striking together of the tongue with the throat, which effort they increase in order to make themselves more intelligible.

2. It is worth noting in these nations a most bilious temperament which gives them a character which is astute, suspicious, bold, haughty, and zealous of its freedom and independence. Their stature varies from group to group, the most impressive ones being those who are born in and inhabit the lands further north. All are dark-skinned, but the natives of the aforementioned areas to the north preserve the distinction of having lighter skin. They are of good disposition and very nimble, with lively eyes, long hair, no

beards, very soft skin, and astuteness and wisdom written on their faces.

3. They are so agile and quick that they rival horses for endurance, outrunning them on rugged or hilly terrain. This is a natural trait which they practice often with the continual movement in which they live, transferring their *rancherías* from one place to another for the purpose of finding new hunting and the fruits necessary to their subsistence. They are sustained as well in this same activity by the vigilance and caution with which they look after their health, which leads them to change their location frequently in order to breathe new air and so that the site which they abandon might be purified. This zeal for preserving their *rancherías* reaches such an extreme that not only do they move them from the site which they occupy whenever someone dies, but even abandon the seriously ill when they feel that they might be contaminated.

# SECTION 4
## Regarding the Lands on Which They Choose to Locate Their Rancherías, and About Their Dwellings

1. All the settlements, or *rancherías* of the nations about which we are speaking are nomadic, except the Navajó, who have maintained a very regular population in ten pueblos[56] in the territory, or province, which they inhabit. In all the others, which should be considered as nomadic groups, the number of persons constituting the tribe bears no relation to the territory which they hold as theirs, or seek to control. Thus one finds empty spaces in such vast lands, and each family father or *ranchería* captain is considered the sovereign of his district.

2. They always judge it more fitting—and choose with good reason—to locate their living sites among very rugged hills and mountains; and consider themselves better or worse situated according to the greater or lesser difficulty of access to their chosen sites. These must necessarily have water and firewood in abundance, the requisite wild fruits, and a natural layout of terrain such that they can barricade and defend themselves against their enemies.

3. Their huts, or *jacales*, are circular, made of tree branches, and covered with horse, cow, and buffalo hides. But the Mescaleros, Lipanes, and many of the Llaneros have tents made of well-cured and very clean skins.

# SECTION 5
## Regarding the Food and Nourishment with Which They Sustain Themselves

1. The Apaches are extremely gluttonous when they have provisions. At the same time, it is amazing how patiently they suffer hunger and thirst in times of calamity and scarcity. Their suffering reaches unbelievable extremes, yet their strength does not falter or decline.

2. The foods with which they sustain themselves include meats, provided by their constant hunting and cattle stealing carried out in the territory of their enemies. Their common sustenance also includes wild fruits that grow in their respective areas. Thus, the latter, as well as the types of game, will vary according to where they are living. But there are some that are common to every place. Among the game are the desert mule deer, white-tailed deer, pronghorn, bears, javelinas, mountain lions, and porcupines.[57] Fruits generally abundant everywhere are the tuna, the *dátil*, the *pitahaya*, the acorn, and the pine nut.[58] One of their favorite treats is also mescal, which comes in several varieties because it is extracted from the heart of the maguey, the *sotol*, the *palmilla*,[59] and the *lechuguilla*. It is processed by being cooked slowly underground until it achieves a certain degree of sweetness and potency. They also make a kind of porridge from the seed of the hay or grass which they collect in great quantities.

3. In the ravines of the same mountains the men seek large and small game, extending their hunts to the adjoining plains. When they have what they need, they carry it back to the *ranchería* and turn the spoils of the hunt over to their women, both to prepare the food and to process the hides which will later be used for several purposes, especially for their clothing.

# SECTION 6
## Regarding Their Clothing

1. One of the peculiarities of the Apaches that first attracts one's attention is their clothing.[60] Once the skins are cured, the men fashion close-fitting garments which leave their arms bare and are short enough not to encumber them for their free and rapid method of travel. Generally they use the chamois derived from the skins of the deer and pronghorn for this purpose. Many of them cover their heads with a bonnet or cap of the same skin, and some adorn these with feathers or animal horns. From the time they can walk they always have very well-made shoes with leggings, which footwear the Spanish call *teguas*.[61] They also wear pendants made of shells, feathers, and small rodent skins, some adding to this adornment by painting their faces, arms, and legs with clay and ochre paints.

2. It is necessary to point out that, although the dress usually worn by the aforesaid nations is the one described, some of them are neater, more fastidious and exquisite in their manner of dress, such as the Mescaleros, Lipanes, Llaneros, and even many of the Navajóos, Xicarillas, and Yutas.[62] Their chamois skins are more finely cured and worked, and most habitually wear good breeches which they make to perfection. Some also adorn their heads with attractive plumage. In short, there is a certain neatness and martial bearing that differentiates them markedly from the other nations, in which dirt and filth are so common.

3. The women's dress is also made of skins, but it differs in that they wear a short skirt tied at the waist and with some fringe at the knees and a shirt or jacket which they put on over the head and which hangs to the waist, covering the breast and back while leaving the sides open. Their shoes are like the men's, and they wear nothing on their heads. They tie their hair in the form of a chestnut, usually wrapping it in buffalo chamois or beaver skin. They adorn their throats and arms with strings of deer and pronghorn hooves, as well as shells, fish spines, and roots of fragrant flowers.

4. The most prosperous and well-groomed families trim their clothing and footwear with porcupine quills, which they soften and

make pliable in order to use it for such finery. Many women also decorate their skirts with a ruffle of little tin bells or pieces of brass, which makes their company quite noisy.

# SECTION 7
## The State of Agriculture, of the Arts, and of Commerce in the Apache Nations, and Their Use of Money[63]

1. The Apache temperament is little suited to agriculture, and with the gathering of wild grains they satisfy their present needs. But several nations, convinced that with very little effort and favored by the fertility of the land they can subsist with greater comfort, harvest some of our grains, of which they are becoming fond. Among the groups that devote themselves more to this natural industry, it is not the men who are employed in this type of work. In addition to the obligations discussed above, women must also carry water and firewood; plant, water, and harvest the cereal crops; tend them until their peak of readiness; and, when these tasks allow time, gather the wild grains.

2. The Coyotero Indians sow a small amount of corn, beans, and some vegetables. The Navajóos, in season, sow corn, squash, and some other fruits and vegetables. They harvest all this in great abundance and keep their stores throughout the entire year. The Xicarillas also plant corn, beans, squash, and a little tobacco in the mountain valleys they inhabit.

3. None of these nations has devoted itself to raising cattle, despite the impressive expanses they have for it. The Navajó nation is the only one that raises wool-bearing and beef stock in some abundance, along with a few horses.

4. The extent of their arts and industry is limited to the thorough curing of the skins in which they dress and which they use in trading at Spanish posts. The best of this work is done by the Mescaleros, Lipanes, Xicarillas, and Yutas, but the Navajóos manufacture frieze, blankets, and other weavings of coarse wool. Not only do these suffice for the consumption of their people, but they take the excess to the province of New Mexico, where they hold trading fairs, ex-

changing their items for what they are lacking, or for other articles which they need.[64]

5. Not long ago money was totally unknown to the Apache nations, and they did not have the slightest notion of its usefulness.[65] If in their raids they robbed some travelers who were carrying money, they took no interest in it, either throwing it away or leaving it, and were only enthused with any other thing that they thought might have some use. Today, they are learning that money makes everything possible, that with it they can obtain many comforts, buying both necessities and luxuries, and that they achieve a freer access to vices. So sure and so convinced are the *indios de paz* of this knowledge—whether in the settlements to which they have been assigned, or passing through our other locales—the first greeting which they make to whoever approaches them is to ask for a *real*[66] or a half.

6. The absence of money is most natural in savage lands, and it was necessity that introduced it many centuries after the more civilized parts of the world were settled. But the most amazing thing is that our province of New Mexico, with more than thirty-three thousand inhabitants,[67] is nearly in the same primitive state. It is absolutely certain that no money circulates in the province and that the aforesaid province claims no more income than the salaries of the presidial company of Santa Fee and the missionaries' stipends, all of which come from the royal treasury in Chihuahua. But this small sum goes for clothing and other effects, and something or another that might take part of their wealth or assets. It is a meager amount which they must keep until they have the opportunity to send it out of the province and purchase whatever their need or whim makes them want. That lovely territory is in such a situation, when it would be quite easy to have currency circulate. This would bring many advantages, the main one being to promote dedication to weaving and wool manufactures, to which those natives demonstrate an ingenious and marked inclination. The worst part is that, in their dealings and purchases, they carry on the most bizarre and wasteful trade, or commerce, in the world, buying and selling at a fixed value without distinction in it between what is good and inferior, and with confusion regarding the supposed value of the peso of the region—it being a quarter of the silver *peso fuerte*—and thus their trade lacks any rational consideration of these differences.

# SECTION 8
## Regarding the Leadership of Their *Rancherías*, the Reasons for Their Relocations, and the Diversions Which They Like Best.

1. To the degree in which the father of a family has more children, grandchildren, nephews, or married dependents, his *ranchería* is larger or smaller, and he is recognized as captain and *caudillo* of it. There are some *rancherías* of eighty and one hundred families or of forty, twenty, or less. Not only does command terminate at the age of decrepitude, but usually all who arrive at a tired old age are the objects of contempt, the butt of ridicule in the *ranchería*. Thus, men or women are esteemed as long as they retain the hardiness necessary to carry out their tasks; but this deserts them late because of their robust character, it being not uncommon to see people over eighty years old participating in the hunt and other strenuous activities.[68]

2. Even though an Apache Indian might be recognized as chief or *caudillo* of his *ranchería*—whether as the son of a captain or through personal influence—the *ranchería* can shrink in size, even though it may be very populous, the moment those who constitute it become discontented and form a separate rancho or join another *caudillo* or tribal captain. Some are so zealous and haughty that they prefer to live totally isolated from the rest, surrounded only by their wives and children, so that no one might challenge their prerogatives as leader.

3. Many reasons have been mentioned why the aforesaid nomadic nations move their encampments from one location to another. They are further obliged to make these moves by another need, which arises when they see that in their current location the necessary food for them and grazing for their horses are becoming scarce. They also consider that they have found some places to be better than others according to the seasons of the year. But these changes of location occur without leaving the mountain ranges that they recognize as their own territory.

4. In a single *ranchería* or in groups of several, their favorite entertainment is dances. Their only music is singing with a pot or gourd,

*Mountain Spirit Dancer.* Watercolor by Allan Houser. (Neg. No. 86228, Courtesy Museum of New Mexico, Santa Fe.)

*Gan Dancers.* Tempera by Allan Houser. (Neg. No. 66814, Courtesy Museum of New Mexico, Santa Fe.)

over which they stretch a tight skin and beat with a stick. To this rhythm, and the accompanying voices of men and women, they all jump together in several circles, with both sexes arranged symmetrically. After the dance begins, repeated breaks occur where two or three of the more skilled and agile enter the circle and do a kind of English dance with great vigor and very difficult contortions.[69]

5. If the dance is being held before setting out to battle, or in celebration of some victorious action, it ends with weapons in hand. Yells are mixed with shots, and without interrupting the cadence of their "*Hó, Hó,*" they proclaim the feats which they have accomplished or which they plan to carry out. There are also dances held by the diviners when they are about to exercise their office. The actors cover their heads with a sort of chamois mask, which they usually adorn with paint, and the dance begins in the manner already described.[70]

# SECTION 9
## Factors That Bring Several *Rancherías* Together, and the Precautions That They Observe for the Security of the Territory That They Cover

1. By chance it happens that sometimes many *rancherías* come together at one place in search of certain fruits that abound in one given location or another. Others are gathered together by prior plan or design with the notion of forming a body for their defense or with the idea of holding one of their ceremonies or where they gather for the hunt. At these ceremonies they often decide upon some plan to attack their enemies. In such instances not only do the *rancherías* of one group combine, but often two or more whole tribes will congregate.

2. In any one of these gatherings, overall command is assumed through common assent by the one with the greatest reputation for valor. But this authority does not instill any particular subordination or dependency on the rest, because each one is free to leave, remain, or disapprove of the plans of the chief. The latter's influence predominates, especially in the preparations of their ground, the method of defense in case of attack, and all other hostile undertakings.

3. Thus gathered, the *rancherías* always occupy the steepest canyons in the mountains, surrounded by the most difficult passes for approaching the site where they are located. That site is chosen, as a general rule, adjacent to the greatest heights in order to command the surrounding valleys and plains. Those who are to serve as lookouts during the gathering locate their camps on these heights, it being their responsibility to watch all approaches and to report immediately everything they observe. It is understood that those employed in such service are the ones with the keenest vision and the most experience and knowledge in war. They are prohibited from making fires while they are carrying out so heavy a responsibility.

## SECTION 10
### Regarding the Great Hunts

1. It has been pointed out that the peaceful activity of the Indian of the savage category called Apache, whether accompanied by others or alone, is hunting. Since we have just discussed their gatherings and the fact that one of their purposes is to make a great hunt, we will relate what is known on this subject.

2. Men, women, and children participate indiscriminately in the great hunts, some on foot and others on horseback. But such a general gathering does not occur for the buffalo hunt, which they call a *carneada*. It requires time and preparations for attack, since they carry it out in territory close to the Cumanches, irreconcilable foes of the Apachería and particularly of the Mescaleros, Llaneros, and Lipanes, who inhabit the lands closest to that type of cattle.

3. Our subject is the hunt in which they usually seek white-tailed

*Hunting Song.* Watercolor by Allan Houser. (Courtesy Philbrook Art Center, Tulsa, Oklahoma.)

*Buffalo Hunt.* Tempera by Allan Houser. (Courtesy Thomas Gilcrease Institute of American History and Art, Tulsa, Oklahoma.)

deer, mule deer, pronghorns, javelinas, porcupines, mountain lions, bears, wolves, coyotes, hares, and rabbits. They reconnoiter the plains, valleys, hills, and mountains which they frequent, and by the tracks and signs that they find they determine the abundance of game existing in the area of search. The captain with the best reputation chooses and orders the day for the undertaking and selects the spots where the different teams of archers—some on foot and others mounted—who are to act as beaters should be in place by dawn, and the locations to be covered by those who are to serve throughout as lookouts to protect against enemy attacks. Only the most reliable ones are entrusted with this duty.

4. In this way, at dawn they have surrounded an area whose circumference usually reaches four, five, or six leagues. The signal to begin the beating and close in is given by smoke signals, to which task riders are assigned. The operation begins by their setting fire to the grass and vegetation all around the circle. Since they are all in their respective positions for this purpose, with torches made from dried *palmilla* bark at the ready, it is only a moment before one sees

in flames the entire circle that is to be beaten. At that same moment they begin to yell and make noise. The game flees but finds no escape, and finally falls into the hands of such clever adversaries.

5. This type of hunt is done only when the hay and grass are dry. In the rainy season, when they cannot burn the vegetation, they set up their encirclements next to rivers and arroyos. They begin the beating with the preparations discussed above, and end up with the same yelling in this second type of hunt, tightening their chosen circle to the very last.

6. A lone Indian will also hunt deer and pronghorns with the greatest skill. He dresses in the skin of either of these two animals which he plans or decides to hunt, covering his head with another piece of hide to hold it so that he can secure it in total comfort and don the head of one of the aforementioned animals. Thus he sets out into the hills, senses from afar where the game he seeks is or might be, and, once he is sure of it, begins to employ his skill with such amazing success that he wastes no shots. He approaches crawling on all fours and mixes in with the closest herd that he encounters. Striking true, he kills in complete safety as many as he can and if they flee he also runs with them. If they panic at the death of one animal, he also feigns a similar panic. With these tricks there are times when he will finish off the majority of the herd that he finds. They especially like this type of hunt for its total efficiency, which is not the case in the noisy scheme of beating, which provides more entertainment than it does efficiency.

7. From the tenderest age they are schooled in this vital activity. When they are boys, the hunting of prairie dogs, ferrets, squirrels, hares, rabbits, badgers, and mice is reserved for them. Through this practice, they develop a very sharp aim and become quite skilled at every type of trick and stealth.

8. They have little interest in game on the wing, but nevertheless, due to a destructive instinct, they kill every bird they encounter with a sure shot. They make little or no use of their flesh, limiting their usefulness to the mere gathering of their plumage, from which they make their adornments, and they have a supply to affix to the tails of their arrows.

9. These nations have not the slightest interest in fishing, despite the great abundance available in their rivers.[71] Yet from time to time they approach the water, kill what seems to them sufficient for the

sole object of keeping the bones for various uses, and throw away the rest. If they would just eat the fish, they would get nourishment with less effort, and with more peaceful activity they could subsist for many days. But at the same time that they have such scorn for fish, they show an excessive passion for the beaver and otter. They consider the flavor and quality of the meat incomparable, and highly prize the use of the hides of both.

# SECTION 11
## Regarding Their Weapons

1. The Apache boasts of nothing more than his bravery, and his zeal on this matter reaches such an extreme that they think less of any man who is not known to have accomplished some feat in war or some other act of valor establishing his reputation. It is customary among most of the groups, especially among the Mimbreño and Gileño, to prefix the title *Jasquie* to one who has made himself known for his daring and gallantry, which is the meaning of the aforementioned word.

2. Before discussing the warfare that these nations conduct, and the cunning and trickery which they use in it, let us give a general idea, founded on purely military principles, of their weaponry and of the differences that exist in this respect between one group and another.

3. Weapons common to all the Indian nations are the lance and the bow and arrow. The latter are placed or carried in a mountain-lion–skin quiver that is slightly shorter than the length of the arrows. Such weapons are not the same in every nation, since they vary according to each one's different way of thinking. The bow is larger or smaller and with different curvatures. The lance is also of a longer or shorter shaft, and the same is true of the arrows.[72]

4. All the Apache nations have adopted firearms, and in their great desire to obtain them they reveal the great advantage of firearms over all other missile shooters when used with intelligence and sufficient ammunition. But the groups most accustomed to their use, and the ones who particularly value them, are the Mescaleros, Llaneros, and Lipanes. The first, who are very bold and spirited warriors, use them with the same skill as they do the bow, and they

are such good marksmen that wherever they sight they place their shot. The Lipanes use them with equal skill, and in order to make more precise shots from horseback most of them have mounted a little fork on the front bow or tree of their saddles, anchored firmly in such a manner that they do not get in the way, and on these they prop their rifles or carbines.

5. In vain has the government of the Interior Provinces of New Spain established a policy prohibiting that the nations on the frontier be given firearms in trade or under any other pretext.[73] It is well known that the English and Anglo-Americans have set up trade with all the savage nations on their borders, and that they only trade with them in rifles, munitions, and one drug[74] or another, in exchange for the furs that both nations so avidly seek. This influx of firearms is sufficient for them to pass through mutual exchanges from one nation to another to the westernmost one. But even if the Indians did not get this type of weapons through contact with our neighbors, who provide them because of the particular advantage that they derive from the aforementioned exchange, and perhaps in order to arm the great number of Indian nations that surround us from sea to sea, they still have another opening through which to receive them, which is our province of Louisiana. All the nations next to it carry on the same type of person-to-person trade with the settlers of that province. And weapons are also provided from time to time on the royal account to all the neighboring nations with which peace treaties have been signed, reaffirming the treaties with express yearly gifts of firearms.

6. The free introduction of rifles and carbines through that province into the hands of the Indians is so well known that the commander of the Interior Provinces of New Spain has often complained and called for its prohibition, to close the door to gifts so pernicious from every angle. Yet the governor of that colony has replied that the donations or gifts of firearms which are made to the nations bordering on the province he commands are the result of having so agreed with the Indians from the time that His Majesty took possession of those dominions, that now denying arms to them could bring dangerous consequences, and that the ends toward which this policy was aimed would never be achieved, in light of the fact that the great influx of firearms came from the Anglo-Americans and the English. That fact would be of greater concern at present than our

eliminating the donations and gifts of firearms which we make to them.

7. We can be sure that the reason why the Indians have not thrown away their bows and arrows when they manage to acquire a rifle is their frequent lack of ammunition and the total lack of means to repair them when they break down.[75] Once they overcame these two drawbacks, which are of the first essence in the continuous use of firearms, the Indians would have no others and would give them unanimous preference, as has been occurring subsequently with every nation in the world that has armed itself with the bow and arrow, through no greater influence–and without attention to the arguments pro and con which have been published on this matter–than the demands imposed by the laws of experience.

8. In spite of the two aforementioned shortages which we are led to believe are the real reason why the Indians have not scorned the bow and arrow, they care for their firearms as much as possible, even when they have no ammunition. And they never lose the hope of finding it by some chance. In the extreme case where their guns no longer work, they still get considerable use from them, using the barrel and other smaller parts to make lance blades, knives, arrow tips, and other tools which they prize highly.

# SECTION 12
## Regarding the Warfare Waged by the Apache Nations

1. Once they have decided on an expedition and entrusted command to the captain who will lead it, they choose a steep ground in the mountains within their own district, with natural defenses and well supplied with water and wild fruits, where they leave their families safe with a small escort. When they set out from there, they separate into small parties. They usually travel on foot in order to conceal their tracks on their route, which they try to make over hard and rocky ground. They reunite at the prearranged time and location near to the territory they are to attack.

2. To carry out their attack they first set up an ambush in the place most favorable to them, then dispatch several small parties of the boldest and swiftest Indians to steal horses, mules, or other livestock in order to provoke the people into pursuing them. They

attack them by surprise and create a bloody carnage. If one of the parties happens to steal a considerable amount before rejoining the ambush or prearranged rendezvous, it will be content with its good fortune and withdraw to the mountains without carrying out the expedition. At other times, not wishing to abandon their plans, they take the best horses for their own use, slaughter the remainder of the herds, and set out to join the others, who are doing likewise.

3. It is impossible to imagine how swiftly they escape when, after a major theft, they take flight for their country. They scale nearly inaccessible mountains, they cross arid deserts in order to exhaust their pursuers, and they employ endless stratagems to elude the attacks of their victims. Far behind on their tracks they always leave two or three of their men mounted on the fastest horses so that they might report what they observe to the rear. If they report that superior forces are coming after the stolen animals, they kill the stock they are driving and escape on the best horses, which suffer the same fate in case they are overtaken, and they save their lives by taking to the rough mountain country. If those in the rear guard report that they are pursued by inferior forces, they wait for them in a narrow pass in a very advantageous position and devastate them a second time. They repeat this trick as often as the occasion permits and the inexperience of their adversaries allows. But if they perceive that their enemies are cautious, wise, and intelligent, they divide the stolen stock into small herds and make their escape in different directions. By this method they are sure to make it back to their country with most of the stock at the cost of some of them possibly being intercepted.

4. When the expedition is concluded and the booty is divided up—in which distribution it is not uncommon for dangerous disputes to arise, to be settled by the law of the strongest—those from each group return to their respective district and those from each *rancheria* to their favorite mountains, without suffering interference from anyone.

5. With fewer preparations and more results, four or six Indians may decide to carry out a sudden raid, which often inflicts a great deal of damage. It is so much more difficult to defend against their ravages as it is easier for them to cover their tracks and sneak into the most distant lands undetected. For this purpose they always make their approach over rugged and rocky mountains, from which

*Fresh Trail—Apache War Party*. Gouache by Allan Houser. (Courtesy Philbrook Art Center, Tulsa, Oklahoma.)

*Ill-Fated War Party's Return*. Watercolor by Allan Houser. (Courtesy Philbrook Art Center, Tulsa, Oklahoma.)

they descend to the vicinity of the villages and haciendas, make their raid with the utmost swiftness, and retreat hastily to the same rugged terrain, over which they continue their trek. It is nearly impossible to find them even when they are pursued with the greatest effort.

6. The times that one sees the greatest bravery, or barbarous daring, of the Apaches is when the occasion arises where they are attacked by their enemies. They never lose their composure, even when they are surprised and have no defense at hand. They fight to the last breath, and members of several groups prefer death to surrender.

7. They act with the same intrepidness when attacking, but with the difference that, if they do not achieve the early advantage that they seek and see the tide turning against them, they are not above fleeing and abandoning their mission. With this in mind, they try to plan their retreat beforehand, and the direction they will take to safety.

8. Only by surprise or by cutting off all escape is it possible to punish the savage nations about which we speak, because if they come to know their adversaries before the action begins, they manage to save themselves with very little effort. And if, despite this, the pursuing parties are determined to smash them, it is at a great risk due to the extraordinary agility which they have and the impregnable crags in which they live.

9. Despite the continual movement in which these nations live, and the great deserts in their lands, the *rancherías* can easily find one another when they wish to communicate, even when they have not seen or had any news of one another for a long time. They all know with unmistakable certainty in which areas the surrounding *rancherías* should be living, according to their well-known familiarity with the mountains, valleys, and water holes that they possess. But smoke signals are their surest mail system, by means of which they communicate with one another. There is no doubt that understanding the smokes is a science, but one so well known to them all that they never mistake the contents of their signals.

10. A smoke made from a height and then stoked higher is a warning for everyone to prepare to contain enemies who are close and have been directly sighted or discovered from their tracks.

Then all the *rancherías* that see it respond with another in the same manner.

11. A small smoke made on the slope of a mountain means they are seeking their own people with whom they wish to communicate. Another in reply made from midslope of a peak means that their people are there and that they can approach freely.

12. Two or three small puffs made in succession in the same direction from a plain or canyon express a request to parley with their enemies, to which a reply is made with similar signals. They have established many general signals of this tenor which are commonly accepted by all the Apache groups.

13. On the other hand, there are also prearranged signals that no one can know without having the code to them, and they use these often when they invade enemy territory on raids.

14. So as not to delay in making the aforesaid smoke signals, no man or woman fails to carry with them what they need to make fires. They prefer flint, steel, and tinder when they manage to acquire these tools, but if they lack these they carry two prepared and well-dried sticks, one of *sotol* and the other of *lechuguilla*. Rubbing vigorously with both hands, with the point of one placed on the flat side of the other in the manner of a small hand grinder, they manage in a moment to light the shavings or sawdust from the rubbed part. This operation is known even to the children.

15. We should not forget to mention the special knowledge they have of the tracks they find in the field. Not only do they determine how long ago the tracks were made, but they can tell whether the horses passed by during the day or night, whether they were traveling freely, loaded, or with riders, and other amazing details that only continuous practice and astute reasoning can make completely clear.

16. Their lack of trustworthiness and ignorance of all laws that govern the waging of war have no other source than the natural propensity of the Apaches to steal and to inflict damage on their enemies. These bad qualities are not aimed precisely at those whom they know as declared enemies, but extend to their having no regard for the property of others among themselves. The powerful take from the weaker with the greatest ease, and bloody disputes are ignited between groups. These come to an end only when a common cause unites them for their own defense.

17. The most irreconcilable hatred that the Apaches hold, and the war that they carry on most tenaciously, are against the Cumanche Indians. This hatred is as old as the nations themselves,[76] and the war is waged with utmost vigor by the groups nearest to them, that is, the Faraones, Mescaleros, Llaneros, and Lipanes. There is no other apparent origin than that both the Cumanches and the aforementioned nations seek to have certain exclusive rights to the buffalo which abound to an astonishing degree on the lands of both sides.

18. No matter how populous a *ranchería* might be, it can make such forced marches on foot or horseback that in a few hours it loses its pursuers. It is impossible to imagine how quickly they strike their camp when they have detected superior enemy forces in their vicinity. If they have animals, these are immediately loaded with their household goods and children. Mothers travel with their nursing infants suspended from head straps in straw baskets, where they are very securely placed, while the men are armed and mounted on their best horses. With the greatest promptness and good order they all head for the place they judge to be best suited to their safety. If they have no transport, then women and boys carry the household goods. The men take up the vanguard, rear, and flanks of their caravan, and choosing the most difficult and uncomfortable ground, they make their migration through the most impenetrable and rugged terrain as if they were wild beasts.

19. Ultimately, in all the marches that they undertake, whether together or separately, the unspeakable mistrust that characterizes them is manifestly at work. Although they may encounter their relatives they take the greatest precautions, which vary more or less according to how long it has been since they last saw one another, and they will not approach a brother without their weapons in hand. They are always on the alert against an attack or ready to commit one. They never greet one another, nor say goodbye, and the most urbane gesture in their society consists of staring at and studying each other for a while before beginning to speak about any matter.

# SECTION 13
## Emotions About the Death of an Apache, Mourning, and Funerals.[77]

1. When the natural or violent death of an Apache occurs, whether it be a husband, wife, child, or relative, the closest kin then show their sorrow by cutting their hair and making other gestures of grief. The horses of the deceased are killed, and all his clothing and property are tossed on a bonfire, to which some others also carry part of their belongings in order to show the maximum grief they have felt. A widower will often refrain somewhat from such extremes due to his other wives who, stricken with jealousy, will claim that he thought more of the dead one than of the present ones. Through these natural principles they convince him, lessen his anguish, and frequently repeat to him a saying which in translation means, "The dead are never mentioned."

2. The cadaver is usually carried to a gully or to a handmade grave. There they toss it, cover it with stones, shout in distraught

*Apache Funeral.* Tempera by Allan Houser. (Neg. No. 66815, Courtesy Museum of New Mexico, Santa Fe.)

voices, and view that site in eternal horror. They feel the same about the place where he died, from which they immediately strike their *ranchería*, never to locate it there again, nor even in its vicinity.

3. In the month of October and part of November of the past year of 1797, I was on commission at the presidio of Janos, which is the most advanced one on the part of the frontier covering Nueva Vizcaya, where several *rancherías* of Apache Indians have been established, with whom we are at peace. I lived those days engrossed in the observation of some people who provided me with so much material for discourse about their barbarous customs, way of living, and enthusiasms. Having witnessed the death and funeral of an Indian in great detail, and greater manifestations of grief than they usually show, I shall relate the incident as unique to this place.

4. An Indian of apparently thirty to thirty-five years of age suffered an illness which, by its severity and its symptoms, those attending him recognized as fatal. Finally toward the end of his prostration, or thinking him near death, they removed him from his hut, laid him upon a large pile of cottonwood branches, and covered him with more branches, leaving only his eyes exposed. Everyone came from his *ranchería* with their arrows and placed them in a circle around the dying man's body. They did the same with their lances, sticking them into the ground not far from the object of their sorrow. At this point a woman appeared—who I learned afterward was the mother-in-law of the dying man—carrying a burning stick in her hand and fixing her gaze on the eyes of her son-in-law. When she saw that one of them had closed, the life of the infidel was considered finished, and she lit the woodpile that was serving as his resting place and covering him. Other women who were also carrying burning sticks set fire at the same time to all the huts in that *ranchería*, except that of the deceased, which they brought in so that it might burn alongside him, as well as his weapons, saddle, his wife's hair, skirts, and other skins that he wore.

5. They let the necessary time pass for the flames to do all their destruction, and the bones that they found among the ashes were taken to be buried on a small, hidden mountain about two miles away from the site where the honorary scene was carried out. At that very instant they moved to a new location from which they could not see the previous one. Then they killed three horses, which were the last remaining property of the deceased, and on the

following day they threw themselves face down in the sand of the riverbed, in which posture they remained without eating or speaking until the third day,[78] when they all arose as happy as they were before the sorrowful event.

6. I tried to inquire into the cause for these strange demonstrations, of which nothing had been reported, but there was no one who could provide the least idea about them. The oldest hands and those most accustomed to dealing with the Indians were as much amazed by them as was the one who had just begun to learn about them through the spectacle of their barbarous funeral ceremony.[79]

*Apache Herdsman.* Tempera by Allan Houser. (Neg. No. 130778, Courtesy School of American Research Collections, Museum of New Mexico, Santa Fe.)

# TERCERA PTE

*Naciones que en el Norte de la América Española deven conocerse por orientales, su caracter, y costumbres: Las caribes de la Costa de Texas sobre el Seno Mexicano idea general de las estable cidas à la derecha del Misisipi. Descripcion del Misouri, con conocimiento de todas las Parcialida des, que avitan sobre sus margenes, y de las inme diatas à los Rios que desembocan en el. De las esta blecidas al O de la parte superior de la Provincia de N. Mexico; de las de la Costa alta de Sonora; de las del Colorado de Californias, y de las que por el NO. siguen hacia el mar, que todas se dan a conocer con el nombre de Na ciones Occidentales*

## Seccion I.

*De las Naciones al Orie. del Rio G. del N.*

1 *Para hablar de las Naciones Gentiles,*

Folio 97, Cortés *Memorias*, Add. Ms. 17652. (Reproduced by permission of the British Library.)

# THIRD PART

*Nations in Northern Spanish America That should Be Known as Eastern, Their Character and Customs. The Caribes of the Texas Coast on the Gulf of Mexico.*[80] *General Notion of Those Nations Settled on the Right of the Misisipi. Description of the Misoury, with Information on All the Groups That Live along Its Shores and on All Those Near to the Rivers That Flow into It. Regarding Those Settled to the West of the Upper Part of the Province of New Mexico, Those of the Upper Coast of Sonora, Those of the Colorado River of the Californias, and Those Which Continue Northwestward to the Sea, All of Which Are Introduced under the Name of Western Nations.*

## SECTION 1
### Regarding the Nations to the East of the Río Grande del Norte

1. In order to speak of the heathen nations that possess most of the vast territory between the Río Grande del Norte and the Misisipi, those that own the banks of the Misoury, those that inhabit different countries to the west, and others that are known as natives of the Colorado River of the Californias, one cannot write with the precise order employed in discussing the Apaches. Of some we have only the slightest information, and of others we have managed–through the most studious and exhaustive investigation–to obtain the minimum necessary information to derive a fair idea of them. We will thus confine ourselves to saying what is known of each particular nation, yet we will point out with total certainty that those for whom we do not report about their customs, beliefs, and superstitions are very similar in all these respects to, or differ very little from, those aforementioned principles written about the Apache nations.

Regarding the Cumanches[81]

2. The Cumanche nation is without a doubt the most populous one known among those bordering upon our farthest provinces of North America. It lives on vast and beautiful lands to the east of the province of New Mexico, and consists of four groups known by the names of Cuchanticas, Jupes, Yamparicas, and Orientales.[82] They are led by a general and a lieutenant chosen by a plurality of votes among their countrymen, recognized by the governor of New Mexico, and approved by the commandant general of the Interior Provinces.[83] The aforesaid general of the nation and his lieutenant are acknowledged and respected by the local captains of each *ranchería*, and all Cumanches offer their obedience to the degree allowed by their constitution and discipline. They listen to the general's advice with the same subordination and follow it in the same good faith that these Indians keep in their treaties. They always tell the truth, understand hospitality, and in general their customs are less barbarous than those of the Apaches.

3. In war they are intrepid and extremely bold in their actions and missions. They are at peace with no other nation but Spain, and carry on a ceaseless war with all their neighbors.[84] The four tribes form a close union. They all love one another, and internal disagreements never amount to more than small disputes, which are settled by the same individuals. They share common interests, and all among them live in an equal state.

4. In their dealings with the Spanish they display notions of honor and of the most rigid justice. He who travels through their lands is lodged, regaled, and treated with the greatest friendship. From the moment the traveler arrives they take charge of caring for his horses and baggage, and if anything is missing at the time of his departure they detain him until it turns up. If it happens that the loss was due to malice, the delinquent is given an exemplary punishment in the presence of the Spaniard. Thus do the Cumanches treat the Spanish travelers who pass through their encampments. On their departure they provide them with an escort to accompany them to the place where the escort can be relieved by warriors and guides from another *ranchería*.

## Regarding the Taucanas

1. The Taucana, or Tuacana, group is settled on the western bank of the Río de los Brazos de Madre de Dios [Brazos River], where it makes its residence in a village of forty to fifty dwellings.[85] It has no more than 130 warriors, all of them mounted. The women and children have the same duties as in the other savage nations, and the dialect they speak is the one common to all the northern groups.[86] They are intimately united and allied with the Taobayaces and Obedsitas, all treating each other as their own people. They are very cruel to their prisoners, putting them to death with tortures that horrify humanity and then devouring them. It is also common among them to leave the dead unburied, and when challenged about this barbarous custom they reply that it makes no difference whether they leave them to be consumed by vultures, animals, and worms or bury them.

## Regarding the Tancagües and Their Allies

1. The Tancagües, who, together with the Yocobanes and Mayeses, form a small nation, live most of the year in the territory next to the Tuacanas on the northern part between the Trinidad and Brazos rivers.[87] They consider their enemies to be the Osages and the Lipán Apaches. They are much inclined to a nomadic life and to stealing, for which they are despised and hated by everyone.

2. The Tancagüe makes war on horseback, like the Tuacana. His offensive weapons are firearms, bows, and spears, and his defenses are the leather jacket, shield, and suede bonnet with horns and feather adornments. The country where they live is perilous due to the frequent raids and invasions of the Apaches, and they are always on the alert against ambushes by them and by their other enemies. They take the greatest precautions, reconnoitering and scouring the countryside before choosing the most advantageous site for their camp. Even though it may be only for a night, they string their sentries at proper intervals to communicate with one another. They exhort one another night and morning to limit sleep so that by dawn everyone is at his respective duties. They travel

very close together and in very orderly fashion so as to prevent surprise.

3.  The captain is never responsible for the outcome of the proposed expedition, nor does he exhort those who gather with him to follow him other than by very calculated discourses in which he seeks to make the strongest case for his plan. If it is decided to set out on campaign, that is preceded by the *caudillo's* fasting, and if it is to hunt or to make some particular journey there is a general fast. In the proceedings and gatherings they speak of the reputation and the good qualities of one another, and in this way they encourage others to emulate and follow the voice of the leader. That is how they enlist or withdraw without leaving either gratitude or resentment, and without creating discredit or scandal. And this exercise of their strange constitution causes not the slightest disruption in the fine harmony in which these Indians live.

4.  On their journeys and expeditions they carry no provisions at all and suffer hunger with unbelievable forbearance. In such cases, they lose their aversion to the most disgusting insects, and with the greatest care they eagerly seek turkey, deer, rabbit, and hare as well as turtle, fox, and rattlesnake. They fill their stomachs with all these, without seasoning or cooking. Thus do they live on such occasions, and as long as they cannot get the food they prefer they mask their hardships with the boisterous gaiety of their dissonant songs.[88]

### Regarding the Taobayaces

1.  Among the nations commonly called northern, that of the Taobayaces is the most civilized.[89] They reside in two villages located on the banks of the Río Colorado de Nachitochez [Red River], facing one another, about 170 leagues northeast of the Tauacanas. The aforesaid two villages probably contain 170 to 180 dwellings, each with a corresponding number of auxiliary structures.[90] The number of inhabitants is close to two thousand; that of armed men, or warriors, is over six hundred. Their dress consists of shirts, boots, and leggings, all of animal skins, and from the same they make their leather jackets, shields, saddle trappings, and campaign tents. To supply themselves with cereals and other produce they undertake very efficacious preparations and preserve them very carefully. Each head of family keeps in his house twenty

or thirty *fanegas*[91] of corn in bull-skin sacks which they make for this purpose. They also make provisions for beans and squash, which they preserve all year long in a very curious fashion.[92] And in addition to these stores, which guarantee their survival with a certain degree of comfort not enjoyed by the other savage nations, they harvest cantaloupes, watermelons, and tobacco in great abundance.

2. In the vicinity of the aforesaid sites there are many springs and perennial fountains of fresh water, enough to irrigate and fertilize the extensive fields where they do their planting. The water of the river is brackish, but its proximity affords them convenient fishing for exquisite and delicious fish,[93] and with that same convenience they slaughter the buffalo and other game that they hunt with no more effort than letting them come to drink. To the advantageous location this nation occupies must be added the nearby availability of all the firewood and timber they need from so-called "Great" forest[94] which extends from the right [east] of the Tuacanas to near the Taboayaces. No canyon or any other break diminishes the breathtaking sight created by the thickness of its luxuriant cottonwoods, ashes, elms, and walnuts, which continue over an area more than eighty leagues long and one to two leagues wide. Finally, so that they might lack nothing, they have in the middle of the river an excellent salt bank whose deposits fill up immediately even when they extract all they want.

3. The beliefs of the Taboayaces are based on recognition of a Creator who lives in the sky, from where he controls everything. They offer him the first fruits of their harvest and hunt, call upon him for success in their undertakings, and observe an infinity of highly superstitious rites. From this type of religious system, which is more rational than what can be found among the other Indian nations, derive more orderly customs, such as the observance of sworn oaths, veneration for the old, humane treatment of the sick, and generosity with outsiders. They live in the belief of the existence of a life eternal where the good will be rewarded–the first rank among these consisting of warriors–and the evil punished by being condemned to live forever among brambles and boulders surrounded by *tigres*[95] and venomous animals. But among these good qualities that distinguish them they have some other very bad ones: they are cruel to their captives, they copulate in the vilest manner, and exhibit other abominable inclinations.

4. Their government is based on a more orderly democracy than that of the Tancagües. Their customs and pursuits are hunting and war. They sustain war continually with two or three nations, and they make their reputations in it, becoming captains through their daring exploits, without regard to any other quality, even though they may be the sons of the most proven leader. To this must be added that pride in their exploits is enhanced by the certain reward of the other life. The lot of women is the same as in other Indian nations: they cure, sew, and paint skins; they fence the croplands; they do the planting and harvest the grains; they cut and tote firewood; they prepare meals; they construct the houses; they raise the children; and their continual attentions do not cease even as they look to the rest and satisfaction of their husbands.

### Regarding the Obedsitas

1. The Obedsitas are a small group living on the eastern side of the Río de los Brazos, about one hundred leagues away from the Tahuacanas.[96] The land they occupy is not as fertile or inviting as that of the Taboayaces, but they are closely allied with the latter and follow all their decisions. They have the same beliefs and customs and, in general, consider each other as a single nation.

### Regarding the Orkoquisas, Vidais, and Texas[97]

1. These three nations are neighbors. The Orkoquisas are settled on the Río de la Trinidad, north of the abandoned presidio of their same name.[98] The Vidais are located from twenty to twenty-five leagues away from them in the aforementioned direction and on the eastern side of the aforesaid river. The Texas are found somewhat above these, also continuing to the north.

### Regarding the Flechazos, the Quitseis, and the Yscanis[99]

1. The first of these three nations is about twenty leagues to the north of the Tancagües on the east side of the Río de los Brazos. The Yscanis are about the same distance away, but to the southeast

and on the west side of the Trinidad. And the Quitseis, or Quicheis, are eight leagues from the Yscanis on the opposite side of the river.

## Regarding the Nabaydachos, the Aix, Saisesdemolida, Nahuchichos, Nazones, and Ynamiches[100]

1. The Nabaydacho Indians are twenty-five leagues to the north-northeast of the Vidais, living on a stream that flows into the Río de Nechas. The Aix are to the east of the Nabaydachos on the east side of the right arm of the Río de Sabinas, leaving the post of Nacodoches eight leagues to the north-northwest. On the east bank of a small river that flows into said arm north of the aforesaid site, and six leagues away, live the Saisesdemolida Indians. Continuing four leagues upstream from them on the bank, one finds the Nahuachichos. Fifteen leagues further up, at the source of the aforesaid arm of the Sabine along the aforesaid bank, one finds the Nazones, and about ten leagues north of that the nation of the Ynamiches is settled.

## Regarding the Nadacos, Quichas, Nacodoches, Guachitas, and Taguayas[101]

1. The Nadaco Indians are settled on the east side of the main arm formed by the Río de Sabinas northeast of the Nacodoches Post. On the same side and ten leagues further up is located another group called the Guichas, and fifteen leagues away, on a stream that flows into the right arm of the Sabinas, live the Nacodoches. About fifty leagues north of the Guichas, and on the east side of the same Río de Sabinas, are the Guachitas. Five leagues away in the same direction and on the same side is located the Taguayás nation.

2. The number of families in the aforementioned eighteen nations that we have just discussed varies slightly from one hundred to one hundred and fifty, and in some cases to two hundred. Their customs are almost the same ones reported for the Taboayaces, Tancagües, and Tuacanas, and they only vary among one or another too insignificantly to be described as more warlike, more civilized, or more extreme in their barbarism.[102]

3. The principal responsbility of the governor of the province of Texas is to maintain the peace and friendship that are preserved with the majority of the nations mentioned above. These go down to San Antonio de Béxar to receive the gifts that are granted to them each year with the approval of the king. This is the method that the authorities have accepted as the most effective in keeping those Indians at peace. But we do not know if this will be sufficient if the Anglo-Americans and English continue the visits they have begun to make to their villages.[103]

# SECTION 2
## Regarding the Carib Nations of the Texas Coast and Adjacent Islands[104]

1. Having thus discussed the nations located or settled within the province of Texas, and others that live outside its borders, it is necessary to tell what it has been possible to learn of the groups on the coast of said province, which is part of the Gulf of Mexico. Those for whom we have information, with good reason to believe that there are no more, are the Carancahuaces, the Cocos, the Cujanes, the Copanos, the Guapites, and the Xaranames.[105] All of them are nomadic tribes, and none would contain even one hundred families. Their character is nothing other than one of atrocious cruelty, treachery, and evil practiced to the highest degree on the poor wretches who have suffered the misfortune of being shipwrecked on the coast, and on the inhabitants whom they have surprised in the interior of the mainland. They have never been observed to remain in a permanent dwelling, and no sooner do they finish one foray than they are planning the next. In the summer they set out from the islands, which are a better haven for them during that season, and in the winter, from the woods closest to the coast. Their weapons are arrows and darts, and their favorite activity is fishing, which provides them their principal nourishment. Most of these groups have taken shelter several times in the missions that have been established for them in response to their requests and false promises.[106] But the only fruit obtained has been their repeated betrayals, when they disappear, committing in their flight every evil that one could imagine. There has been too much docility in giving

in to their insistence that missions be founded for them. These have been abandoned every time one has been established for them, resulting in a considerable waste of the expenditures funded by the royal treasury for such purposes, and a multiplication of the number of apostates—far too great in the aforesaid class of savages—because of the ease with which they have been administered the Sacrament of Baptism. Such examples, and the long experience which we have with the Carib Indians of the coast, should leave no doubt as to the course we are to adopt toward them, which is either to settle them in missions in the interior, far from the coast, or to exterminate them, sparing no one but the innocent young. The latter course, though it may seem horrible, is well founded on the principles and goals of what should be understood as true humanity. Their murderous nature and vicious character offer no hope, and from their treacherous lips come no whoops of joy except when they are stained with the blood of the unfortunate shipwrecked and with that of the wretched inhabitants of the sparsely populated province of Texas.[107]

2. Their women do not have reason to be as industrious or as active as those of other nations, because among them there is no cultivation of land, and the nudity in which they all live relieves them of that type of work. But they participate with the men in the fishing and in handling the paddles of the small canoes in which they make their forays from the islands to the mainland, and from the latter back to the former.

# SECTION 3
## Regarding the Nations to the Right of the Misisipi;
## Description of the Misoury and Information on the Groups That Live on Its Shores

1. Some of the nations about which we are going to speak live in the interior of Louisiana, others to the north of it on the shores of the Misisipi, some along the rivers that flow into that river's lower reaches, and the greatest number along the banks of the Misoury and the shores of the streams that feed its waters. In order to give

the most reliable idea of what is known of them, we will proceed in the same order, providing the most information possible on the lands and sites that each nation inhabits, and of the relations that they maintain between them, with the clear understanding that much of the information given in this section was compiled from the repeated journeys of the French when Louisiana was in their possession, and other reports that we have managed to obtain after said colony was ceded to the Spanish Crown.[108]

2. The Misisipi flows into the Gulf of Mexico at 29° 7' north latitude, and thirty-two leagues upstream on the east bank is the city of New Orleans, capital of the province of Louisiana. Twenty-eight leagues above there one encounters on the west bank the mouth of the Río Colorado, by which one proceeds to Nachitóchez, a post very near to the province of Texas. The Ouachita River flows into said river, and there are no more than twelve leagues between the former and the Misisipi by the waters of the Colorado. In the intervening territory live the Caudachos Grandes and Pequeños, Yataces, Adaes, Nachitóchez, Rapids, Pacanas, Alibamones, Chatos, Ochonias, Biloxis, and several other groups of lesser importance.[109]

3. Continuing the ascent of the Misisipi to 180 leagues from the mouth of the Colorado, one finds the mouth of the Río de San Francisco de Arkansas on the same west bank. Twelve leagues up the latter is the fort named for Carlos III.[110] Between it and the aforesaid Misisipi, at varying distances, are found the villages of the Arkansas, known by the names Ogapas, Otoius and Tulimes.[111] Continuing up another one hundred leagues, one encounters the Pequeños Osages.[112] These are all the nations on the right side of the Misisipi which are considered to neighbor closest to the Interior Provinces of New Spain.

4. Continuing the ascent from the Pequeños Osages, one reaches the settlements of Santa Genoveva and San Luis,[113] which are twenty leagues apart and about five hundred leagues from the city of New Orleans. San Luis is where annual gifts were distributed on behalf of His Majesty to the Sius, the Grandes Osages, the Ayués, Cancés, Panis-mahás, Saex, Autodatas, Hotós, Pequeños Osages, Misurys, Renards, and the Kas-Ka-Kias.[114]

5. We have arrived at the point where we must discuss the Misoury. This is a great river that has its source in the mountains to

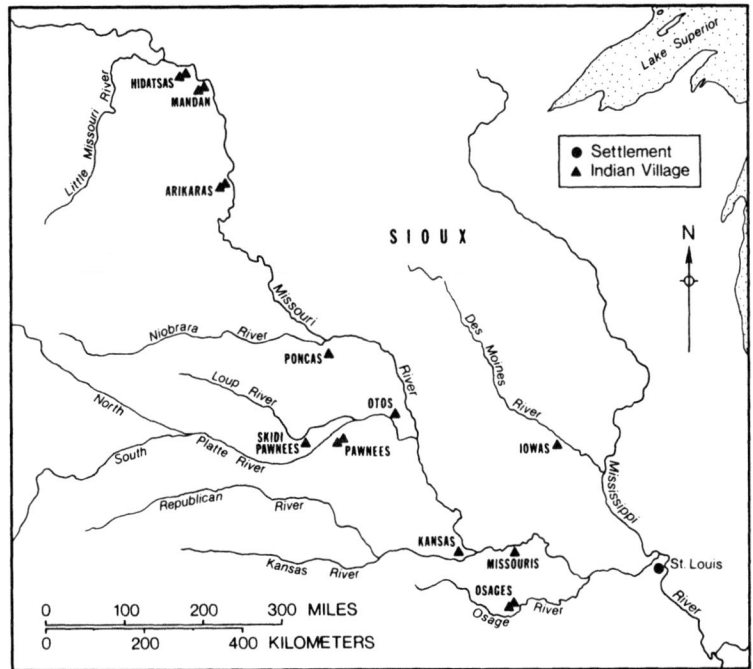

Nations of the Missouri. (Map by John V. Cotter.)

the north of the province of New Mexico, descends from the northwest, and flows into the Misisipi at 40° north latitude, and five leagues above San Luis de Ylinoa. The aforesaid river has a swift current and is full of shoals along its length. Its navigation is hazardous for this reason, and because the driftwood that is caught on the aforementioned shoals makes the current flow more swiftly. Thus, when the floods subside there is hardly passage for a canoe, and the channel varies almost every year.

6. In the trade which the French and a few Spanish have carried on along the Misoury, they have never penetrated more than two hundred leagues up from its mouth. The English, who have newly established themselves in that area, regularly penetrate further.[115] Leaving for the time being their explorations and relations, we will relate some recent and undisputed reports that have been communi-

cated to us by the Ris, or Arricara,[116] Indians. They affirm that two hundred leagues above their villages there is a great cascade that falls from a high mountain they call "the singing mountain," from the noise of the water as it falls.[117]

7. Before proceeding, and in order to understand the information we have regarding this subject, it is necessary to point out that the mountains that form a cordillera from the northern fringes of New Mexico to the east create the high, mountainous country between said province and this part.[118] From these mountains some of the rivers that originate in that direction flow into the Arkansas, which has already been discussed, and the rest into the Misoury. All the streams originating west of the aforementioned mountains flow into the Río Grande del Norte.[119]

8. The Misoury cuts through this chain of mountains north of the source of the aforesaid Río Grande, its own source lying to the west-northwest.[120] According to all the ancient and modern reports that have been compiled, the great cataract, or cascade, about which the Arricaras speak is formed in the cut the river makes through the aforementioned mountains. This is all we know about its course, and what has been theorized about the waters that flow into it, because, while we speak about those tributaries with greater certainty, it is through conjecture and without the proof called for by any positive statement. We will limit ourselves to providing information on the part of the aforesaid river that has been traveled, and on the known rivers that flow into it.[121]

9. Two leagues from the mouth of the Misoury, to the right of the river, there is a rock or island which they call Aguafría.[122] It is about one-half league in diameter and some two hundred feet high. In some places it slopes in the manner of a very gentle ramp, and there is a meadow with good lands on which to build settlements.

10. It is two leagues from Aguafría to La Aldea de los Suis.[123] The latter site is a great meadow which begins one-quarter league from the left bank of the Misoury and continues to the east to the Misisipi. The land is very good and ideal for cultivation and, furthermore, there is the lovely advantage of having two leagues from the aforesaid Aldea de los Suis a coal mine[124] which can be exploited at little cost. And from the mine to Puntacortada, on the same bank, it is another two leagues.

11. Continuing seventeen leagues from Puntacortada along the aforementioned bank one finds a channel which the French call "El Canal del Pensamiento," and at this point is the mouth of the Río de la Lutra,[125] navigable by canoe in the driest seasons for thirty or forty leagues. Ten leagues further up is the Hahá, thought to be fifty leagues from San Luis.

12. From El Canal del Pensamiento to the Río Gascomade[126] it is two leagues. The Gascomade discharges through the right bank of the Misoury thirty leagues from where the latter enters the Misisipi. Its shallowest waters are navigable for fifty leagues, and during its deepest flow, for more than 120. About thirty leagues from its mouth, one approaches the branches of the Maramek,[127] which empties into the aforementioned Misisipi six leagues below the aforesaid post of San Luis.

13. From the Gascomade to the river of the Grandes Osages[128] it is ten leagues or, rather, forty from the mouth of the Misoury on its right bank. It is a river of considerable size. It descends from the west-northwest and one can travel up it to the village of the Grandes Osages, located 120 leagues upstream, although it is necessary to wait until the waters have begun to rise, because in the dry season it is impossible to proceed beyond the Río de Nianga,[129] which feeds the waters in great abundance. From its mouth up to one branch that flows into it fifteen leagues below the aforementioned village, there are eighty-nine islands,[130] there being a great number of these, as well as falls, to be found all along it. They are the principal cause for its turbulent and swift current. It is also subject to great floods from the many rivers that flow into it.

14. On the same shore and about three leagues further up from the mouth of the Río de los Grandes Osages there is a small river called the Cedros,[131] because of the many trees of this type that grow in the vicinity of its shores, and which generally have a circumference of from two to two and one-half *brazas*.[132]

15. On the aforementioned left bank of the Misoury, and twenty leagues above the mouth of the Río de los Grandes Osages, one finds the mouth of the Mina,[133] which name was given to this small river because of the many salty springs that flow into it.

16. From the Río de la Mina to the Charaton it is eight leagues. The Charaton is two twin rivers, which discharge from the left bank

of the Misoury at a very short distance from one another,[134] and which come very close to the Río de los Frayles,[135] which empties into the Misisipi.

17. It is eight leagues from the Charaton to Río Grande.[136] The latter flows over a distance of nearly three hundred leagues, paralleling the Misoury for some forty leagues. It comes very close to the Río de los Frayles; from the great island that lies eighty leagues up it, one can reach the Río Grande in two days' travel, and the Misoury in two more.

18. From the Grande to the Río de Cans, or Cancés,[137] it is thirty-four leagues. The Cancés discharges through the right bank of the Misoury, 108 leagues from the mouth of the latter. During high water it is possible to ascend it to the village of the Republic of the Panis,[138] whom the other Indians call Paniguacy, or "partridge eyes." Then comes the Nichenanbatone[139] on the left bank of the Misoury, near the Río de los Frayles, and ten leagues from the Nichenanbatone is another little stream named Agua que llora.[140]

19. After the Cancés comes the Río Chato,[141] which is one-half league wide, and although it is one of the largest of the rivers emptying into the Misoury, navigation on it presents many obstacles and problems. It is believed to originate in the mountains of New Mexico, and according to what the Indians say, it has many full flowing branches. But we only know it up to the great island eighty leagues from its mouth.

20. Penetrating fifteen leagues from this site on the right of the Misoury, one finds the village of the Auctocdatas,[142] and at a short distance, that of the Panis.[143] Three leagues above this latter village, and on the left shore of the aforesaid Misoury, is the mouth of the Río de Papas, or Lobos, and thirty leagues from its mouth are the settlements of the Lobo Indians, or Panis-Mahás.[144]

21. From the Chato to the Río de los Suis[145] it is thirty leagues. The latter discharges through the left bank of the Misoury, and it is affirmed that twenty leagues up it is the quarry of red stone from which the Indians make the pipes for their *cahunetes*.[146] It is about one hundred leagues from the aforementioned Río de los Suis to the one they call the Escarpado. It is wide and dries up in the summer, but its waters flow down swiftly in the spring, for which reason the Indians also call it the "river that runs."[147] It is thought that about ninety leagues from the Arriacaras it descends from the west-north-

west[148] and has its source in the mountains of New Mexico. A league below its mouth there is a small river where the village of the Poncás Indians is located. All the country between the Chato and the Escarpado is prairie with sandy soil.

22. About forty-five leagues above the Escarpado is the Little Misoury, which is nothing other than the first branch of the river of this name. Its navigation is difficult and its source is in the aforesaid mountains of New Mexico. The Pados,[149] or Toquibacos,[150] live near it or at least they have there some small forts to which they retreat. From the Little Misoury to the first village of the Arricaras, it is no more than forty leagues.

23. From the Escarpado to the Arricaras the country is quite arid and nearly treeless, rocky and full of sand hills. But from the Arkansas River to the cascade about which we have reported there is an expansive prairie, traversed and watered by the rivers that have been mentioned. These fertile prairies border on the west with the mountains of New Mexico, on the east with the western shore of the Misisipi, on the south with the Río de San Francisco de Arkansas, and on the north its borders are unknown because the Indians who have given the most accurate reports have not ventured beyond the "singing mountain."

24. This is such an enormous expanse of territory that its climate is necessarily varied. Certainly nowhere else does one encounter such a variety with regard to the latitude of each location. The proximity of the Canadian lakes, the uncultivated territories, and the immense prairies do not present the slightest barrier to the north winds, which, along with other physical causes, make these lands much colder than those of the same latitude in Europe. Its abundant waters and lands and its extensive prairies formed by nature are the reasons the territory is filled with buffalo, pronghorns,[151] deer, wapiti,[152] and other species. The woods are full of game and are particularly abundant in ducks, turkeys, *faysanes*,[153] etc., and the land is generally ideal for the cultivation of wheat, flax, and hemp.

25. Informed of the reports that we have been able to acquire in order to give a brief description of such vast lands, which one day can be the theater of many events that will attract the attention of Europe and of America, let us move on to discuss the different Indian groups on the shores of the Misoury and of the rivers that empty into it, which was the principal object that we set forth.

26. The village of the Grandes Osages[154] is located 120 leagues up the river of that name. Two leagues from its mouth, on a large prairie greatly elevated in one part, is the most populous nation among those with whom we have dealt on the Misoury. They may have five hundred men capable of bearing arms, and as a rule all are good hunters.

27. The Pequeños Osages,[155] to whom those who have settled on the upper Río de Arkansas belong, have their village eighty leagues from its entrance into the Misoury, on the right bank on a large meadow about a league away. They can field from 250 to 300 warriors and are skilled hunters.

28. It is important to observe that, although the normal activity of the nations of the Misoury is hunting, they base their wealth on the possession of many horses, which they obtain from the Laytanes, or Apaches,[156] and from the frequent thefts by some nations from others. What is more amazing is that, with the great number of horses and mares they have, they totally prevent the breeding of these animals, overloading the latter and running them too much.

29. The lands in which the Pequeños Osages do their hunting are those lying between the Río de la Mina and the Río de los Grandes Osages, and their game consists of deer, wapiti, bears, mountain lions,[157] beavers, and otters.[158]

30. The Misurys,[159] who are a league away from the Pequeños Osages, have their villages on the banks of the Misoury. There are about 150 warriors. They are at peace with the Pequeños Osages, because of their close proximity, and with the nations of the upper Misoury, in order to obtain horses. The limits of the Misurys begin at the Río de la Mina, extending upward to the Fire Prairie[160] eight leagues below the Cancés on both banks of the Misoury. They hunt the same game as the previous groups.

31. The Cancés[161] have their villages 140 leagues from the mouth of the Misoury, on a very high bank half a league from the right shore of said river. Their warriors would number probably 250 men, and they are without a doubt the best hunters. They maintain peace with the Pequeños Osages and Misurys, and they make war on the Panis in order to obtain horses. Their hunting grounds extend up the Cancés to the Ninahá.[162]

32. The Hotos[163] live on a small hill in the midst of a prairie up the Río Chato, fifteen leagues from its mouth. There are about 120 warriors. This nation is the only one on the Misoury that has no need for trade, or commerce, with San Luis de Ylinoa, since they have a close friendship with the Ayués,[164] who are settled along the Río de Frayles and who trade with the English and Anglo-Americans.

33. From the aforementioned Río de Frayles it is possible to make an easy and swift invasion of the upper Misoury and the province of New Mexico, opening a path through the Ayués and Hotós, with the guarantee that the latter are in control of the Gran Río, two days' march from the Misoury. And from the first of these two groups to the great island, which is in the Río de Frayles eighty leagues from its mouth, takes only two more days of travel. Thus, as has already been suggested, the Americans from the other side of the Misisipi would have to travel no more than two or three days in order to find themselves on the banks of the Gran Río, or rather in Hotó territory. Its passage would not only be a great threat to the upper Misoury, but it would also make it possible for the Americans to win over the Panis-Mahá nation, leaving them with free and safe travel through the extensive territory inhabited by the aforementioned nations.

34. During the past twenty-six years English traders have entered the villages of the Panis and the Hotós several times.[165] With this familiarity, and without there being presently any other nation to watch over their ambitions than the Anglo-Americans who have extended their power in that area to the east bank of the Misisipi, it remains to the free will of these traders or to that of the others settled recently on the banks of the Misoury, to put into practice every plan and policy they see fit to establish their control over that country or to undertake whatever their ambitious notions might suggest to them.

35. The Panis[166] are situated twenty-seven leagues from the Río Chato, and they have from 400 to 450 men capable of bearing arms. They do their hunting in the territory that lies between their river[167] and the Chato, and they go out from their villages as far as the Río de San Francisco de Arkansas.

36. The Panis-Mahá[168] are located thirty leagues up the Río de

Papas, or Lobos,[169] counting from its mouth. There are about 350 to 400 warriors. Their own hunting grounds extend from the left bank of the Chato to that of the Pados, which is a branch of the Papas, and throughout the territory lying between their villages and the Boyer.

37. The Poncás have a village on the little river below the Escarpado. Nevertheless, they are nomadic and fierce in nature. They kill without mercy anyone they encounter and attack furiously any time they feel they have the advantage. But when they do not, they attempt to make friends with those who—were they fewer in number—they would treat with the greatest cruelty. They have no more than eighty warriors, and maintain friendship only with those whom necessity forces them to hold as friends.

38. The seven villages of the Arricaras, or Ris,[170] are located along the Misoury about four hundred leagues from its mouth. There are about one thousand warriors, and although they inhabit an extensive territory, they have no horses because the arid and barren land does not produce the necessary pasturage.

39. In times past the Pados were the most populous nation in that area, but the wars that they have carried on with the others have decimated them, such that they have come to the extreme of consisting of no more than four small remnants whose structure saves them from the fury of the other nations, which hate them intensely. Despite the tenacious persecution they suffer, they are thought to have more than 350 warriors who are very skilled with bow and arrow and fleet of foot.[171]

40. The Laytanes, or nomadic Apaches,[172] live in the chain of mountains northeast of New Mexico and are held to be the best warriors along the Misoury. They dominate all neighboring nations, and although they are divided into several bands or small groups, they all live in unity and enduring friendship.

41. Los Suis,[173] who extend from the Río de Frayles to the source of the Misisipi, are like the Laytanes, that is, the dominant nation on the left shore of the Misoury. No other Suis than those who trade on the Río de Frayles get to San Luis. They are nomadic and live divided into different groups.

42. The Higados-duros or Pitacóricos[174] are settled along the upper Misoury above the Arricaras. They constitute seven important villages which make a large population, but there is no more infor-

mation about them than the reports given by the Ris Indians and other nations. Because of this lack of information we will not attribute a number to the Laytanes, Suis, and Pitacóricos, as we have done for the other tribes we have discussed in this section.[175]

# SECTION 4

## Regarding the Nations to the West of the Upper Portion of the Province of New Mexico and Those of the Upper Coast of Sonora[176]

1. The province, or territory, of the Moguis Indians, or Moguinos,[177] is to the west of the capital of the province of New Mexico. This nation revolted toward the end of the seventeenth century, driving the Spanish and missionaries from their pueblos. No formal attempt has been made since then to subjugate them by force, nor is there any hope of achieving it by the gentle persuasion that has been employed on several occasions. The pueblos in which they are settled and established are seven, named Oraibe, Tanos, Moszasnavi, Guipaulavi, Xongopavi, Gualpi, and another small one without a name located between the latter and Tanos, but whose inhabitants are colonists subordinate to the pueblo of Gualpi.[178]

2. The Moguinos are the most industrious Indians of all those who inhabit and have been discovered in that part of America. They cultivate the land with great dedication; they harvest the same grains as among all the civilized peoples of our provinces; they take care never to lack vegetables; they have as many fruit trees as they can obtain, with a particular abundance of peach trees; and in all their fields they make use of the proper tools for cultivation. They possess and raise with meticulous care both large and small livestock. They have looms for the coarse weavings that they wear. They are very jealous of their freedom. They do no harm to the Spanish who pass through their pueblos, but they are very careful to see to it that they leave immediately.[179]

3. The aforementioned pueblos are built with great regularity: the streets are wide and the dwellings of one or two stories. For their construction they raise a wall about a *vara* and a half[180] above

the ground floor, which is the level of the terrace and the pavement of the lower section, up to which they climb on a wooden ladder that they remove and put back as often as they need to climb up or down. In the terrace, onto which all the doors of the lower section open, there is a ladder to climb to the upper, whose configuration consists of a main room and two or three additional rooms. And in the same patio there is another ladder to climb to the rooftop or second story, if there is one.

4. Their government derives from the cacique of each pueblo, and for their defense they all make common cause. Their native people are of a lighter[181] color than that of the other Indian nations. Their dress differs little from that worn by the Spanish Americans of those remote provinces. Their saddles are the same, and their weapons are the lance and the bow and arrow.

5. The women dress in a full-length tunic, without sleeves, and a black, white, or colored shawl in the manner of a mantilla. They cinch the tunic with a sash, which is usually of several colors, and they do not wear beads or earrings. The old women wear their hair divided into two braids, and the young ones in a bun over each ear. They are fond of dances, which are a frequent source of diversion for them and in which the only music is a jar that they beat with two sticks and a kind of shepherds' flutes.[182] For these gatherings, which are their occasions for greatest display, there is no Mogui of either sex who does not wear a head dressing of attractive feathers.

### Regarding the Seris, Tiburones, and Tepocas[183]

1. The Seri Indians live toward the coast of Sonora, in the famous Serro Prieto[184] and its vicinity. They formed a very populous group that wrought great havoc in that rich province. They are cruel and bloodthirsty, and with their poisoned arrows they took the lives of many thousand of inhabitants, also causing the failure of the expedition against them planned in Mexico. Today they are thought to be reduced to a small number, they have been attacked with success by our troops on many occasions, and they are restrained by the vigilance of the three presidios established for that purpose. None of their customs has the aspect of civility, and their beliefs and marriage exist under the aforesaid barbarous notions that have been mentioned with reference to the most savage nations.

2. The Tiburones and Tepocas[185] are a more numerous tribe, and of greater importance than the Seris. But their bloodthirsty character and customs are the same. They usually reside on the Ysla de Tiburón, which is joined to the coast of Sonora by a narrow underwater isthmus, which they cross by swimming at high tide; at low tide the water reaches only to their waists or below.[186] They go to the mainland, where they raid and steal, then return to the island. This is the reason that their brazenness usually goes unpunished. Twenty-three or twenty-four years ago His Majesty approved and ordered the execution of a plan to destroy them on their own island, but up to the present season it has not been attempted. For that purpose troops are being trained in Sonora. Their expedition is supported by a corvette from the department of San Blas and two or three smaller vessels, all to carry landing forces from the permanent companies of that port in the Mar del Sur. The array seems somewhat overblown, and the forces amount to such a great number that certainly not one-third of them would take part. And despite everything, we must fear that the Tiburones and Tepocas will not be finished as is believed.

### Regarding the Pimas, Papagos, and Cocomaricopas[187]

1. On this side of the Gila, covering a territory that extends to what is considered the frontier of the province of Sonora, are settled the Pimas Gileños, or rather the Pimas Altos.[188] It is a nation of 2,500 souls who live in the towns of San Juan Capistrano, Sutaguison, Atison, Tubuscabors, and San Seferino de Napqub. They are affable and close knit. They dress in cotton and wool cloth which they make. They cultivate the land and harvest cotton, wheat, corn, and other cereals, for whose irrigation they have well-constructed *acequias* and each landowner encloses his field. They raise horses, sheep, and hens. Their weapons are the ones common to the Indians, and generally they are at war with the Apaches and with one nation or another of the Colorado.

2. The Papagos, who are a nation of four thousand souls, inhabit the farthest frontiers of Sonora, on the lands nearest the sea up to near the mouth of the Colorado River. They speak the same language as the Pimas, and dress in the same manner. They are divided into several *rancherías*. Their customs are the same, and in their

friendships and conflicts they always act in accord with their neighbors.[189]

3. The Opas Indians, or Cocomaricopas,[190] as they are commonly known, live in the area beyond the Gila near the Río de la Asunción.[191] They number over three thousand souls, who populate several *rancherías*. They speak the language of the Yumas. They are of the same character as the Pimas and dress the same way. Without need for irrigation, they harvest all grains twice each year. And in all other respects they differ little from the Papagos and Pimas, with whom they live in great harmony.

## SECTION 5

## Regarding the Nations of the Colorado River and Those Which Continue to the West and Northwest to the Coasts of Alta California

1. The Cucápa[192] nation is of some three thousand souls who live scattered among different *rancherías* established to the right of the Colorado River from 32° 18′ upward. On the opposite side and eleven leagues to the northeast begins the Jalliguamay[193] nation, which consists of two thousand inhabitants. They are very generous, of a lighter color than the other nations of this area, and fastidiously dressed. The Cajuenches,[194] who total three thousand souls, live on some very delightful lands on the same side as the Jalliguamais and very near to them. These three nations reap abundant harvests of corn, beans, squash, cantaloupes, and watermelons. The Cajuenches are inclined to fishing, and at times it provides their subsistence. They are of a happy disposition and entertain themselves with the dances which are their most celebrated festivities. Both the people from this nation and the Jalliguamays array their huts in the fashion of encampments, surrounding them with stockades in order to defend themselves against a surprise or against a sudden strike that their enemies might attempt.

2. The Yuma[195] nation consists of three thousand souls, who are settled on the right side of the Colorado. They are neighbors of the

Cucapas, and their southernmost *rancherías* begin at 33°. They are more civilized than the three nations that have just been discussed, and they harvest the same crops in abundance.

3. The Jamajabs[196] have the same number of people as the Yumas. They are located on the left of the Colorado between 34° and 35°. This is the best of those nations known to be natives of this famous river. They neither create disturbances nor steal. They show much spirit and are extremely courteous. The men go about totally naked with nothing more than blankets or rabbit or otter-skin cloaks, which they obtain from the nations of the west-northwest. They make a show of this lack of covering during the hardest part of winter, insisting that it makes them hardier. Indeed they are so, and stoically suffer hunger and thirst for three and four days. They are very healthy and quite presentable. The women have more art and grace than those of the other nations, and dress in skirts and over-blouses like the Yumas. Their speech is quite strange; they speak in arrogant and uninhibited shouts, and in their arguments they slap themselves mightily on the thighs.

4. The Jalchedums[197] live on the right side of the Colorado, and their *rancherías* begin at 33° 20'. They have the same customs as the other nations on the lower part of this river.

5. The Cucupas, Jalliquamays, and Cajuenches have the same language while the Yumas, Jalchedums, and Jamajabs have another, with the difference that these latter accompany their arguments and expressions with the arrogant gestures that have been mentioned.[198]

6. As a result of the reports and visits made on repeated occasions by several missionary fathers to the nations of the lower Colorado, manifesting and reporting the favorable disposition and desires of all those Indians that missions be established for them, a royal order was obtained for this to be carried out. Prior to this favor, the principal captain of the Yumas, named Palma,[199] was in Mexico [City] and, along with many of his people, received the Sacrament of Baptism. They returned for the establishment of their desired missions, which were founded among them late in the year 1780 under the names of Nuestra Señora de la Concepción and San Pedro and San Pablo del Vincuñer. But soon they grew impatient with the missions for which they had longed and before the year was out they had destroyed them, treacherously murdering four missionaries, the troops of the protective guard, and settlers who were to be

the first colonists to develop those new towns. They took the women and children captive, but during the expeditions that were organized to punish them most of the captives were freed. Since then we have heard nothing of the nations of the Colorado River, which, because of their distance, cause no harm in the province of Sonora.

7. Twenty leagues' journey to the west-¼ northwest of the Jamajab nation begins that of the Benemé.[200] They are very effeminate Indians, and the women are not very clean. Their clothing is nothing more than cloaks of otter and rabbit skins. The country in which they live has good pasturage and delightful woodlands. They have a great abundance of wild vineyards and meadows covered with hemp. This nation is very populous and extends to near the coast. They are peaceful and courteous to outsiders, the principal demonstrations of their generosity and kindness being the tossing at travelers of many white shells, which they collect on the beaches of the Sea of Californias,[201] and of acorns that grow in their woods.

8. In the mountains to the northwest of the Benemé and about thirty leagues' distance from where this nation terminates, are the *rancherías* of the Cuabajais.[202] Most of these form a great square with two portals, one to the east and the other to the west. The distribution of the square is in divisions made by arched tree limbs, which usually are willows, and a small number of windows opening to the outside so that smoke may escape from the different fires around which each family is encamped. In the two aforesaid portals they keep sentinels during the night. All the country over which this nation's *rancherías* extend is very pleasant, fertile, and covered with trees. And what is most agreeable about these Indians at first sight is their order and cleanliness, in which aspect they far surpass those of the Benemé nation.

9. Twelve leagues north of the last *ranchería* of the Cubajai nation, and on the banks of a copious river, begins the nation of the Noches Indians,[203] whose lands are most fertile, covered with trees, and as extensive as one might imagine. Said nation is very friendly and affectionate. Its Indians are very presentable and the women the best groomed and cleanest. They take good care of their hair, dress in chamois skirts and skin cloaks, and their favorite and continual pleasure is to bathe in the abundant rivers of crystalline waters that

surround them on all sides. In this nation they also use the bath which they call the Temascal,[204] which is an underground chamber covered in the fashion of an oven and with a small door in the roof or on the side. When they wish to bathe they light a fire before entering it, and since there is no more ventilation than the aforesaid little doorway, they sweat copiously after a short time of being inside. Thus they remain until they can take it no longer, then they run out and plunge into the river where they bathe thoroughly. It should be understood that the Noches' habit of frequent bathing makes them so clean that they stand out among all the nations and branches of Indians. This is also probably the cause of the delicateness they have about traveling on foot.

10. All the vast country containing the Sierra Madre of the Californias, with its eastern and western slopes to the sea coast, is occupied by nations of savage Indians, some more numerous than others. The principal qualities and customs that constitute their character are, for the most part, the ones common to all Indians, with little difference in their level of civilization, except to add that they are more peaceful and of a better disposition. We have met some of them and heard news of others through the groups of that region with whom we have dealt from time to time. These include the Cuñeil,[205] bordering on the post of San Diego, whose rancherías continue on to the mouth of the Canal de Santa Bárbara.[206] The Quemeyá[207] nation also borders on the aforesaid post of San Diego and on the first nations of the aforementioned channel mouth. The Jecuiche[208] nation has its settlements near the Puerto de San Carlos,[209] and the Jeniqueches[210] border on the Jalchedums and the mission of Santa Ana. The Cuñeil and Quemeyá nations each have their particular dialect, and the other two speak the same language as the Benemé. The Cobaji[211] nation and the Noches also have different languages, and the first one borders on the east with the Chemeque nation, and on the west with the second one.

11. In the great expanse lying between the Gila, the Colorado, and the southern part of the province of the Moquis, there are several nations which have not been reconnoitered or visited as have those of the Colorado and those ones in the Sierras of the Californias whom I have treated in some detail. But it is known that in the aforementioned territory there live many tribes, most of them

nomadic. The number of souls each is thought to contain is very small. All of them are Yavipais[212] to which generic term is added another designation in each case. Those about whom we have information because of contacts with one or another of them, and through reports about some of them, include the Yavipais-tejuá, who have their own language, the Yavipais-muca-oraive, who also speak a different language, and the Yavipais-abema,[213] Yavipais-cuernomache, Yavipais-cajuala, and Jaquillapais,[214] who speak a single dialect. To the north of the Colorado River live other groups who can be considered a single populous nation. They are the Chemeque-cajuala, Chemeque-sebinta, Cheme-quaba, Chemeque, and Payuchas.[215] All of these speak the same tongue, with the exception of the Payuchas,[216] who speak differently.

12. We have word also that to the north of these last nations are established others which are called the Guamoa, Guanavepe, Guallivas, Aguachacha, Japiel, Baquioba, and Gualta.[217] In none of the aforesaid nations, nor among any that are known in the northwest of America, is there detected the slightest notion of religion, nor reason to assume them to have any formal idolatry. But in general they do distinguish and respect those held to be sorcerers, which is a natural trait in the character of all the Indians.

# SECTION 6
## Regarding the Nations to the North-Northwest of the Province of New Mexico

1. The exploration which for the Spanish has shed the most light on the nations that live in the north of America is the trip made in the year 1776 by the Reverend Padres Fray Francisco Atanasio Domínguez and Fray Francisco Vélez Escalante. After having seen the summary of the detailed log of this successful expedition, I had the good fortune to meet and talk with the Reverend Padre Domínguez, a priest of very worthy ideas, great integrity, and well-recognized virtue. He said—in a most natural manner, and with that enthusiasm that accompanies truth when it comes from those who can never stray from it—that about two hundred leagues to the

north-northwest of the villa of Santa Fee in New Mexico, he encountered the Indians called Yutas Zaguaganas.[218] Among their
several *rancherías* there are six lakes which in their language they call
Timpanogotzis, or Timpanocuitzis,[219] of which the first is found at a
latitude of 40°. Continuing about 120 leagues to the west of said
lakes, one comes to the great Valley and Lake of the
Timpanotzis,[220] the home of the most docile and friendly nation of
all the ones we have come to know in the New World. The aforesaid valley begins at 40° 49' of north latitude. It contains in its
center a great lake which not only is fed by many streams and
creeks, but is watered by four rivers that flow through the valley at
proportionate distances and empty into it. Thus it is possible to
establish there a rich province abounding in every kind of crop and
livestock. One sees much brotherhood in this nation, and a most
sincere disposition to receive religion. They engage in hunting to
provide themselves with skins, and although they use the meat in
their meals, fishing is their main delight, and it sustains them in
abundance and without the slightest effort.

2. Traveling from the lake of the Tampanotzis toward the southwest about thirty leagues, one encounters another populous nation
with thick bushy beards.[221] Some of their beards are so long that the
old ones look like the ancient anchorites. They also have the nostril
pierced near the outside edge, and in the hole they wear a small
bone of a deer or other animal. Not only for their beards but in their
physiognomy as well they are similar to the Spanish. The docile
nature of this nation is the same as that of the Lagunos, or Timpanotzis, and they bade farewell to the missionaries with the most
expressive demonstrations of affection. They showed great emotion
at their departure, to the extreme of shedding tears. The name of
these Indians in their language is Tiransgapui,[222] and the valley
where they live begins at 39° 35' north latitude.

3. The expedition returned through several nations bordering on
those of the California coast, then went down to explore the Colorado, and followed the route of the Moqui and Zuñi to Santa Fee.

4. This report—attested to by two friars of recognized merit and
by the other individuals who made up the escort that was assigned
to venture into such distant lands without any idea or knowledge of
them—gives sufficient basis to destroy the argument of some writers
who, in discussing the Indians, have set forth as a common principle

in their descriptions of these nations that the Indians had no beards, only because it was true of the ones that they had seen or heard about. It is true that among the majority, that is the first thing one notices. But it is also true that among some, more than others, one sees many men with thin beards. And lately we know that there are nations of Indians with beards as thick and bushy as those in the provinces of Europe where men are more distinguished by this notable feature of their face.

5. The same can be said for the mythical existence of the city of Quivira, whose grandeur and population are the hallucination of many who neither know where it is nor have seen any report giving information about that civilized city in the northern regions of America. Not only that, but in many maps that I have held in my hands, the dreamed-of Quivira occupies a determined spot on the globe, while they ignore the placement of well-populated locales in the middle of the provinces that we have ruled since the early days of the conquest. I do not categorize Quivira with the questions about the celebrated Binaspore[223] in India, and with a more certain judgment I venture to deny its existence, sighting, and reports made about it. Let us observe and read with care the detailed logs of the difficult journeys made in the past thirty years by the Reverend Padres Fray Francisco Garcés, Fray Francisco Atanasio Domínguez, and Fray Francisco Silvestre Vélez Escalante as well as several other priests and military leaders who have entered those remote lands. And let us examine the journeys also made to them by the Reverend Padre Fray Juan de la Asunción in his trip of the year 1538,[224] by Captain Francisco Vásquez Coronado in the year 1540, and by Don Juan Oñate in the year 1604.[225] These explorers of long ago were apparently the ones who told of the great city of Quivira, and having looked at the reports of the rivers they encountered, the distances between them, and the directions the explorers took, we have learned that the Río de las Balsas which they recorded is the Colorado of the Californias, and that the other information that they compiled was about the river we now know by the name of San Felipe[226] and the other Grande[227] mentioned by the Noches Indians and other nations in that region. We know the same about the numerous groups dressed in skins and chamois that inhabit those regions. Doubtlessly, the populous and walled Quivira

would be some pueblo like that of the Moqui, which might have been destroyed with the ease that many Indian dwellings are torn down, or it may continue to exist, along with others, as do the seven pueblos of the aforementioned Moqui territory.

## The End

# EPILOGUE

The abrupt, rather lame conclusion of the *Memorias* and the crudeness of the complementary map attest the conflicting demands that befell Cortés with his transfer to Mexico City. Then the largest metropolis in the New World and second only to Madrid in all the Spanish empire, Mexico City was already famed for the baroque grandeur of its public and private buildings. But the late eighteenth century found the viceregal capital enjoying a great new burst of public construction in the neoclassic style, fostered by its second Viceroy Conde de Revillagigedo. Engineer Cortés, with his specialty in building, could hardly have wished a more stimulating professional environment.

Officers of the Royal Corps of Engineers had long figured importantly in the civil as well as the military architecture of New Spain's metropolis. The most senior and most prominent, Col. Miguel Costansó, had been active there for more than a quarter of a century; Lt. Col. Manuel Agustín Mascaró had worked closely with Constansó in Mexico City for a decade, until assuming command of the engineers at Veracruz in 1795.[1] Lieutenant Cortés also would find in Mexico City challenges more suited to his training than those of the northern frontier. His response entailed handsome architectural drawings: a few survive in Mexico's National Archive, allaying such doubts about his draftsmanship as might arise from his unpolished map.

The most important of his commissions came in 1800 from Viceroy Félix Berenguer de Marquina, who ordered Cortés to design long-contemplated barracks for a full regiment of dragoons, to be constructed on land between the Paseo de Bucareli and the Casa de la Acordada.[2] Although it was a very large project, Cortés delivered the drawings, with full explication and cost estimates, just six months later in June, 1801. His covering letter to the viceroy is in a polemic but tactful vein, somewhat reminiscent of the introduction of his *Memorias*. Tracing the history of the problem from an initial royal order in 1783, Cortés rehearses the deplorable conditions under which the dragoons have lived and worked for want of appropriate facilities and strongly urges that the viceroy brook no further delay in meeting their pressing needs.[3] Perhaps his historical bent

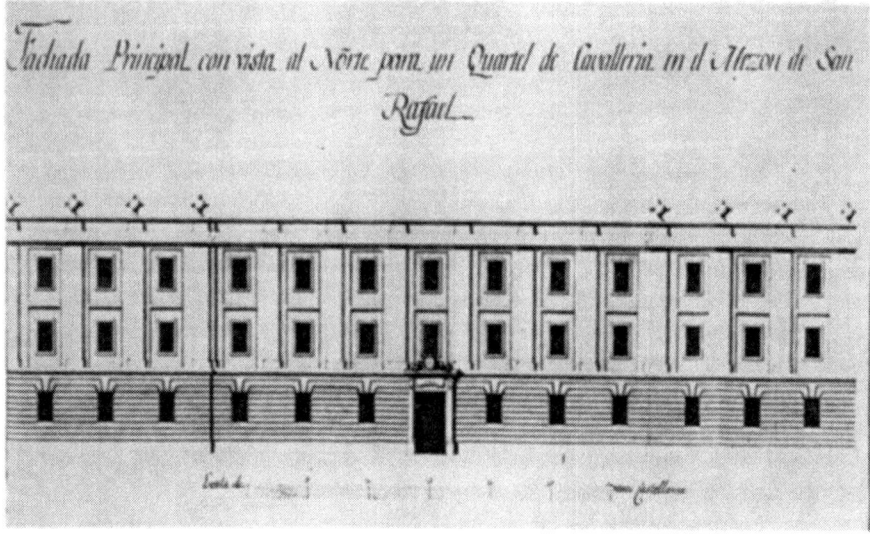

Architectural drawing by José Cortés, 1801. (Courtesy Archivo General de la Nación, Mexico City.)

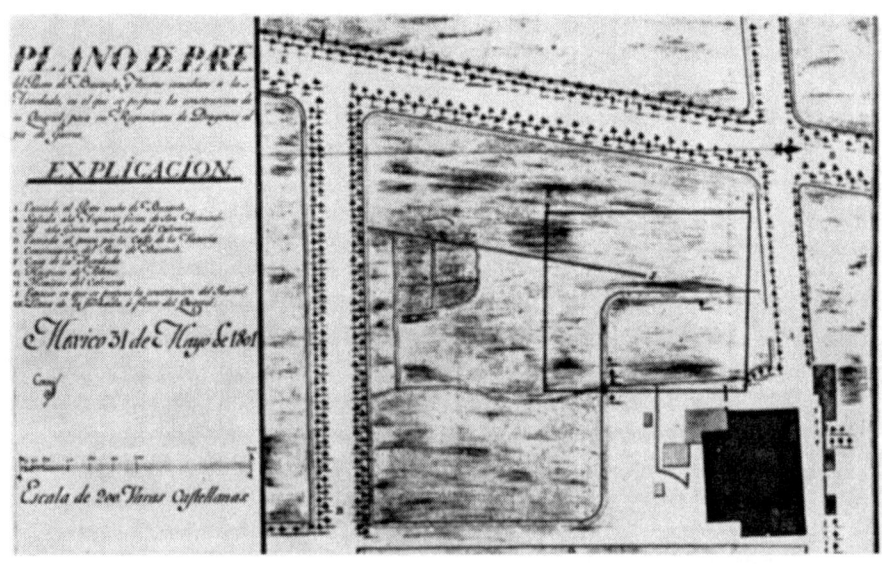

Site drawing by José Cortés, 1801. (Courtesy Archivo General de la Nación, Mexico City.)

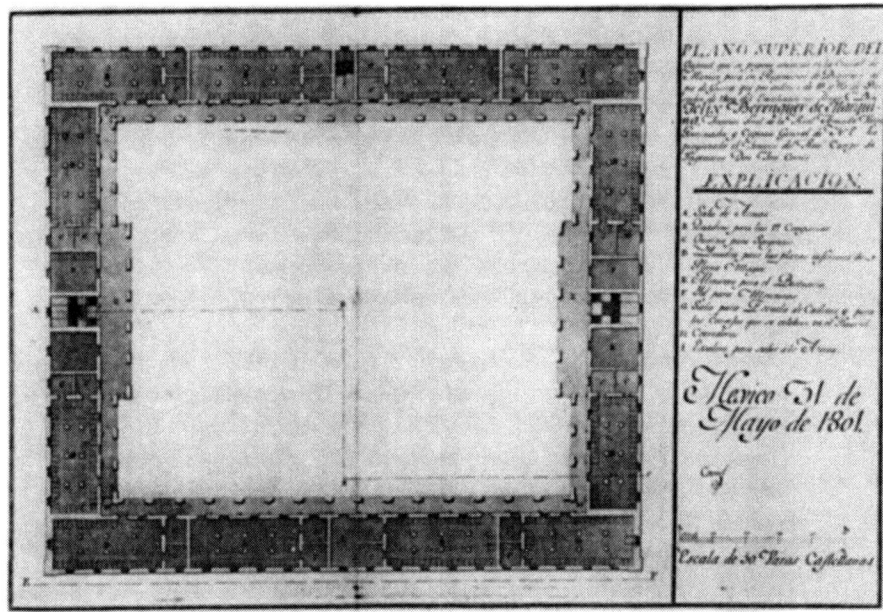

Architectural Drawing by José Cortés, 1801. (Courtesy Archivo General de la Nación, Mexico City.)

and his concern for Apaches led Cortés also to ponder the Casa de la Acordada, which loomed over his barracks site. Over several decades, and as recently as 1797, that grim prison had been the destination, often final, of occasional clusters of Apache prisoners deported from the northern frontier as incorrigibles.[4]

The year 1802 began auspiciously for Cortés when the general of the Corps of Engineers recommended, and the king approved, his petition for reassignment to Europe, noting that he had served the required term in America. By the time he was posted to Cádiz in June, 1802, Cortés had received his captaincy. By March, 1805, he was Lieutenant Colonel Cortés. By November, 1807, he was also designated Sargento Mayor de Brigada, and was a member of the Royal Engineers' *Junta Superior*, the committee of five high-ranking officers responsible for evaluating all proposals for fortifications and other new works for defense in Europe and the Indies.

Exhilarating through his return home to Andalusia and his rapid promotions must have been for Cortés, those were disquieting years. Cortés had barely returned to Cádiz before Spain's appallingly weak king, Carlos IV, signed Louisiana over to Napoleon's France, only to have it sold to the United States within a year. What a monstrous example of the attrition of Spain's North American possessions, against which Cortés had warned so emphatically in his *Memorias*! Imagine then his chagrin at seeing the minister most responsible for the Louisiana folly thrust upon the proud engineers as their titular head. In 1803 the queen's lover, Minister Manuel de Godoy, added to his pretentious title of Prince of Peace that of Generalissimo of a reorganized and somewhat diminished Royal Corps of Engineers.[5]

Insult and injury seemed unending. Early in 1808 Napoleon's army invaded Spain. An indignant Spanish populace forced the hapless cuckold Carlos IV to abdicate in favor of his son Fernando VII, only to find both father and son held captive in France by Napoleon, who thrust his own brother, Joseph Bonaparte, upon the Spanish throne. The outraged people of Spain contemptuously rejected the spurious king, governing themselves with local juntas, and rallying Spain's forces—formal and informal—against the French invaders with surprising effectiveness. The Iberian peninsula soon became a principal theatre of the Napoleonic wars, with British armies campaigning against the French in occasional loose concert with the Spaniards. A Central Junta emerged to govern Spain and the overseas empire in the name of Fernando VII until *El Deseado* could return to the throne. First Seville and then Cádiz functioned as the seat of national government while Madrid endured some six years of French occupation.

As a specialist in fortifications, Lieutenant Colonel Cortés found himself in the thick of the military preparations from the outset, working with local juntas at the cost of considerable exasperation. The Central Junta of Talavera de la Reina called upon him in 1808 to fortify their city, which would be the next major target of the French armies on their projected march from Madrid to Lisbon. Cortés completed that job by mid-December, 1808, then returned to his regular assignment as commander of the engineers in Extremadura. He found his responsibilities for the fortifications of that critical region on the Portuguese frontier greatly complicated by controversy with the Junta of Badajoz, and suspected that their complaints about him were unfairly holding up his promotion. The Central Junta, then acting at Seville for the absent king, reassured Cortés of their full confidence and ordered him to continue his command in Extremadura.

Happily, within half a year Cortés was posted to the more congenial environment of Cádiz, in charge of fortifications at that key citadel. His responsibilities entailed much more than improving the long-established shoreline fortifications. Now, with Napoleon's forces rampaging about the peninsula, Cádiz had to brace for possible attack by land as well as sea for the first time in centuries. The local populace rallied enthusiastically to the challenge, so Cortés found himself directing civilian volunteers in the swift construction of new walls to gird Cádiz against overland invasion.[6]

There, at the temporary hub of Spanish government, Cortés pursued personal as well as career concerns. In June, 1809, he obtained the crown's permission to marry Doña Catalina Ximénez Bretón y Landa and promptly did so. They occupied suitable apartments in the Casa de Ingenieros, a handsome seaside building reserved for lodging officers of the corps who were stationed in Cádiz or in transit to or from assignments in the Americas.[7] The next spring found Doña Catalina heavy with child.

In addition to the responsibilities of his own new household, Cortés pursued the duties of executor for the estates of his mother and brother. The brother, Manuel Cortés y de Olarte, had died in December, 1807, in Managua, where he was senior canon of the Cathedral of Nicaragua and acting head of the diocese. But for two years thereafter, José María was unable even to obtain a copy of the will that named him as the canon's principal executor. Then their mother, Doña Juana Olarte, died, also having designated José María as principal executor of her estate. At Cádiz, in January, 1810, he petitioned the king–in reality, the Central Junta–to direct Guatemalan authorities to help him expedite his discharge of the executor's duties imposed by both estates. The commanding general of the corps forwarded that petition with his endorsement. Apparently the response was encouraging: in March, Cortés directly petitioned the Audiencia of Guatemala for the pertinent documents.

The spring of 1810 brought Cortés an important new assignment to the command of the Royal Corps of Engineers in Mallorca. He delayed his departure from Cádiz, ostensibly to facilitate an orderly transition of command to his successor, but perhaps also to await the birth of the child expected in June. During that waiting time, in the course of his duties on the fortifications of Cádiz, Lieutenant Colonel Cortés suffered such a hard fall that survival seemed impossible, so grave were his head injuries. He received last rites and was carried home to die. Weeks later, on June 1, he lay there yet, helpless, in a coma much of the time, his head and right side virtually paralyzed, his life still in grave doubt.

That day Doña Catalina received from the captain general of Andalusia a verbal demand to vacate immediately the Cortés apartments in the Casa de Ingenieros, which was suddenly required to lodge officers and cadets of a new military academy. Moving Cortés was unthinkable. Doña Catalina balked, launching a vehement petition to the king to protect her helpless husband and herself and their unborn child against the captain general's arbitrary authority. She begged that they be allowed to remain in their quarters until Cortés could undertake his journey to Mallorca. The head of the corps supported her, verifying that any move would threaten his injured officer's life.

Within two days the Central Junta, acting for Fernando VII, requested the captain general not to insist upon removal of the Cortés family. Greatly embarrassed by accusations about inhumane treatment of an injured officer and a woman in advanced pregnancy, the captain general insisted that he had actually offered another house and defended his demand as necessary to implement the royal order establishing the new military academy. But he relented.

Within a month, either divine Providence or time, quiet, and devoted care turned the tide for Cortés. Still subject to dizziness and very clumsy in movement, he was not yet fit for duty, but he felt well enough to travel to the famously therapeutic thermal baths of Cartagena. On July 5, 1810, Cortés signed with a firm hand his petition to the king for the requisite permission. Endorsed by the head of the corps, the petition was promptly granted: two months with full salary to go to Cartagena to take the thermal baths to recover his health. In mid-July Cortés sailed from Cádiz with his family.

Their summer voyage along the Costa del Sol should have been recuperative. Instead, pirates captured them off the Cabo de Gata and dumped them on a deserted North African shore, stripped of all their money and possessions, even their clothing. They were rescued, together with other victims, by the Spanish vice-consul at

Orán, who shipped all of them on to Cartagena. Although destitute, Cortés and his family somehow continued to the vicinity of Murcia where he began the baths. Fellow officers urgently reported the family's plight to the leaders of the corps, who in September and again in October petitioned the Crown for prompt relief to Cortés: at the very least, payment of four months' salary due him, preferably supplemented with special subsidies for his subsistence and cure.

Whether or when help reached the beleaguered family is uncertain. Lt. Col. José María Cortés died at Murcia on January 4, 1811. Of the fate of his wife and child, there appears no record.[8] But his curious *Memorias* survived to weather an odyssey of their own, as strange as that of their author, and so earned for Cortés a little niche in the intellectual history of his time.

The principal agent of the *Memorias'* survival was the internationally recognized geographer, naval Capt. Felipe Bauzá, whose own speciality was mapping. He had served as cartographer on Malaspina's great scientific expedition to America, Asia, and Oceania in 1789-94, then played an active role in the development of the Spanish Dirección Hidrográfica, also called the Depósito Hidrográfico. When established at Madrid in 1797, the bureau's primary responsibility was nautical science, particularly the collection and creation of maps and charts, but its broader mission included collection of maps, books, and manuscripts bearing upon the history of discovery and exploration, ethnographic data, reports of natural phenomena – in short, the whole range of scientific inquiry opened by Spain's vast enterprises around the globe, on land as well as sea.[9]

Bauzá assumed directorship of the Dirección Hidrográfica in 1809 under conditions of grim emergency. His initial challenge was to escape Madrid ahead of the rapacious French invaders, moving to Cádiz all that he could transport of his agency's collections and equipment. Bauzá continued the activities of the Dirección Hidrográfica at Cádiz until restoration of the rightful monarch and the end of the war permitted the bureau's return to Madrid in the autumn of 1814. Bauzá's vigorous leadership of the bureau continued until his equally vigorous service as Mallorca's representative to the Cortes from 1821 to 1823 attracted the fatal displeasure of the restored Fernando VII, forcing him to flee. Late in 1823, Bauzá embarked from Gibraltar in a British warship to seek refuge in London. He anticipated only a brief exile until reason could prevail, but the stubborn despot placed his foremost geographer under a death sentence that ruled out any return to Spain until the king should relent or die. For eleven years Bauzá played an active part among his scientific peers in London, faithfully working on his maps by day and writing by night, assiduously cooperating with his colleagues in Spain, and ever poised to return to family and homeland at the earliest opportunity.[10]

The Cortés *Memorias* were caught up in the Bauzá odyssey. Their geographic and ethnographic content were precisely the kind of material that Bauzá collected, both for the Depósito Hidrográfico and for his own substantial library. The *Memorias* may have come to his attention in Madrid, either through the high command of the royal engineers, or through direct contact with Lieutenant Colonel Cortés, whose duties with the *Junta Superior* of the corps took him there in 1807 and 1808. There is even greater likelihood that the two scholarly officers knew each other in Cádiz, where both served in 1809 and 1810. Cortés was just five years younger than Bauzá, and their common scientific interests could well have made them congenial acquaintances. Whether as a personal gift or through an official transacton, Bauzá acquired at least one copy of the *Memorias* and the accompanying map, both of which would remain among his personal possessions.

Bauzá took some of his instruments and essential books and documents with him on the British brigantine that carried him from Gibraltar to England. Afterwards he relied upon friends to send him many more that he had left behind. Specifically, in May, 1824, Bauzá asked to be sent the diary of Padre Font[11] to facilitate the California Gulf portion of the geography upon which he was working, and also one or two volumes of diaries from Santa Fe and others dealing with geography and travels. Moreover, he asked for whatever there was in his boxes that might appear potentially useful for his project. Late in July he received three boxes, short a few items that he had especially wanted and now specifically requested again. He was still working on the geography of North America and wanted more books, positions, and maps correcting the western coast.[12]

It seems most likely that the Cortés *Memorias* and map were among the materials that reached Bauzá in London in July, 1824, there to remain for a decade. In the autumn of 1833, within a month after the death of Fernando VII, the succeeding government of Isabella II granted the sixty-year-old Bauzá amnesty with restoration of all his rights, ranks, and honors. But a stroke seized the fine old scholar in the midst of his preparations to return home, and he died in London on March 3, 1834.

The British government, well aware of the scientific treasures possessed by Bauzá, promptly sought to acquire his collection. But his family was reluctant to see that legacy in foreign hands, and so agreed to a counter proposal from the Spanish Crown. With the official condolences came a request that the papers be turned over to Her Majesty's minister to England, who would arrange transport of the fifteen chests that Bauzá had packed for the voyage to Spain. Some of the materials would be reclaimed as belonging to the state, but the Crown meant to compensate the widow for Bauzá's great services to the Spanish nation.

In fact, no compensation materialized, and Bauzá's fifteen boxes lay quite neglected in the Ministry of State at Madrid until his widow deemed it prudent to retrieve them as a precaution against losses. In 1844 Don Francisco Michelena purchased from the family for a modest sum all of Bauzá's collection on the geography and hydrography of America.[13] In short order Michelena offered the materials to the British government. Prime Minister Robert Peel himself pursued the matter and determined that the documents had no current naval or political value to Great Britain but might be appropriate for the British Museum. There was some doubt about appropriate price: given the official position of the original collector of the papers and maps, it seemed likely that copies of all the documents were still in the Spanish archives, which would materially lessen their monetary value and also in some measure their interest.[14] The British had yet to comprehend that Bauzá had saved for posterity many manuscripts of which no other copies survived the Napoleonic wars and subsequent turmoils in Spain.

Michelena pressed the British Museum for a decision in the spring of 1845, warning that he had received a proposal from Venezuela for part of the collection and a tentative overture from France as well. He was determined to seize the moment, while questions of the annexation of Texas and the Oregon boundary issue made Bauzá's documents more interesting than they might ever be again.

Once Michelena satisfied the questions of the Peel government about the legitimacy of Bauzá's ownership of the collection and its final relinquishment to his heirs by the Spanish government, they struck the deal that would make the British Museum a treasure-trove of Spanish history and cartography.

So Bauzá's copy of the Cortés *Memorias sobre las Provincias del Norte de Nueva España* and the accompanying map came to rest in the British Museum, as Add. 17,562 and Add. 17653c, respectively, in the Manuscripts Department of the division now called the British Library. The reverse of its title page bears the neatly penciled notation, "Purchase of M. Fr. Michelena y Rosas, 2 Dec. 1848." It is a workmanlike leatherbound manuscript volume of roughly octavo size, its 142 folios handsomely lettered and occasionally ornamented in a hand which may be that of Cortés himself or that of a professional scribe. The title page bears the notation "N° 5"; thus far, there appears no way to determine whether more than five copies were made or what were the circumstances of their creation. No other copy of this apparently original series has been discovered. In the public archives of Spain and Mexico there appears to be no trace of the Cortés *Memorias* at all, except a microfilm at the Museo Naval in Madrid of Bauzá's copy now held by the British Library. Perhaps other manuscript copies survive in private collections in Spain.

One other copy of the *Memorias*, of very different character, also rests in the British Library as Add. 13,989. It is a small, nondescript volume of 157 folios, poorly lettered on inferior paper and indifferently bound. A previous owner's notation on its title page explains that this is a copy of a manuscript owned by Brigadier Joseph de Urrutia of the Royal Corps of Engineers, who died in 1800, only a year after Cortés completed the work. That is a useful bit of information, confirming that the *Memorias* speedily reached the highest level of the corps. Oddly incomplete, this copy omits the Preface, which was vital to the purpose of Cortés. A further oddity is that it is bound together with a response to an inquiry from the London Society of Antiquaries to Spanish authorities concerning the location in southern Spain where Julius Caesar defeated the forces of Pompey at the battle of Mundo in 46 B.C. That problem was assigned to an officer of the Royal Corps of Engineers, who reported that the action occurred near Ronda.[15] There appears no clue to the circumstances of the creation of this curious volume, which belonged to Don Juan Perez de Villamil before it passed into the collection of Lord Kingsborough.

Certainly the Cortés *Memorias* caught the fancy of nineteenth-century manuscript collectors and dealers. One of the keenest competitors in that arena was an American, Obadiah Rich, who served as U.S. consul in such prime collectors' venues as Valencia and Madrid while conveniently maintaining a thriving book dealership in London. Spanish manuscripts enjoyed a great vogue, sometimes to the point of mania, among British and American collectors, a market to which Rich catered most successfully. For a decade both Bauzá and Rich moved in London's circle of connoisseurs of rare books,[16] a connection that may account for three showy renditions of the Cortés *Memorias* now found in the United States. Bauzá's severe financial straits may well have led him to permit, or even to undertake, for a suitable fee, copying from his own documents for the collectors' market.[17]

All three of the lavish specimens presently identified in the United States append to the Cortés *Memorias* the 1776 diary of the Journey of fathers Domínguez and Escalante which figured so importantly in the text of Cortés.[18] While it was a logical choice with respect to unity of subject matter, the economics of the collectors' market probably inspired the addition. The diary's length–somewhat greater than that of the *Memorias*–padded the content enough to support the big, elegant folio format for which collectors would pay handsomely.

Of the three, the most interesting history belongs to the copy that came "home" to the northern Borderlands region–now Southwest in the parlance of the United States–that spawned the *Memorias*. Obadiah Rich sold it first to Edward King, Viscount Kingsborough, a passionate collector of manuscripts pertaining to Mexico. Kingsborough's mania for documents was a major factor in his unhappy end in 1837 in Dublin, where he died in prison for debt. Of his manuscripts, which were sold with all possible dispatch by the Dublin booksellers Hodges & Smith, some went to Rich, who in 1843 offered thirty of the volumes to another obsessive collector, Sir Thomas Phillipps.[19] Rich described them as "modern copies, all made expressly for Lord Kingsborough in Spain, under my direction." He also remarked that he had duplicate copies of several of them, which he expected to sell to an American library. Phillipps accepted all thirty at ten pounds per volume, but subsequently accused Rich of having transcripts made of them for the American market and refused to pay. A sordid round of suit and countersuit followed, and it was not until January, 1849, that Rich received final payment.

So that rendition of the Cortés *Memorias* became Phillipps Manuscript 11636, one among the most astonishing and important array of rare books and manuscripts ever amassed by a private collector. Eventually, in 1919, it turned up at Sotheby's to be auctioned in one of the century-long series of sales of Phillipps manuscripts. The catalog described number 328 thus: "Bound by Hering in blue Morocco, richly gilt, with the arms of Lord Kingsborough on the sides. 536 pp. folio, 1799." Apparently it sold to another private collector or dealer, for it came back on the London market in 1955, when the catalog of Maggs Brothers Ltd. featured it as number 1233: "IMPORTANT UNPUBLISHED MANUSCRIPT ON NEW MEXICO AND THE SPANISH NORTH-WEST." An alert librarian at the University of Arizona, Barbara Paylose, spotted the item and the university promptly cabled an offer, disgruntling a number of American dealers who contacted Maggs too late.[20]

Hence this most widely traveled specimen of all known copies of the *Memorias* rests on the old Apache frontier as manuscript number 40 in the Special Collections Library of the University of Arizona, in fine condition, still sporting its blue morocco and gilt, with the arms of Lord Kingsborough.

Another of the three is in the New York Public Library, where it is number 92 of the Rich Collection. It was one of a fabulous lot of Spanish rarities that Obadiah Rich offered in 1848 through aggressive Vermont dealer Henry Stevens, who scoured Europe as agent for several rich, ambitious American collectors. Many of the books went to John Carter Brown. James Lenox paid six hundred pounds for a veritable treasure-trove of manuscripts, including one of the elegant folio volumes combining the Cortés and Domínguez-Escalante documents. The lot dwelt virtually inaccessible in Lenox's private library in New York City for nearly four decades before passing in 1897 to the Manuscript and Archives Division of the New York Public Library.[21] As with most other volumes in the same lot, Rich had this copy handsomely bound in red morocco with gilt. Of its 214 folios, numbers 1 through 98 contain the Cortés *Memorias* and 99 through 214 the Domínguez-Escalante diary. The style of its title page, its size, and its format are the same as that of another copy now in the Library of Congress, although the pagination differs. Comparison of the two led analysts at the Library of Congress to conclude that they were made with the same criteria or by order of the same person in the nineteenth century.

Time has been less kind to the Library of Congress copy, which now wears a tan buckram binding, probably of post-World War II vintage, with "Library of Congress" lining and end papers.[22] Folios 1–88 comprise the Cortés *Memorias*, folios 89–171 the Domínguez-Escalante diary. It was in the library of Col. Peter Force, which the Library of Congress purchased in 1867. Force was said to have acquired it in London (presumably from Rich); its history before that was a mystery to official Washington in the mid-1850s. A penciled notation on the upper right corner of the title page, "no.22," conveys no meaning today.

Force's copy of the Cortés *Memorias* came to public attention after a reconnaissance mission took another young lieutenant, Amiel Weeks Whipple of the U.S. Army Topographical Engineers, into the Apachería in 1853. That was the era of the great search for the optimal route for a transcontinental railroad, and Whipple's task was to explore the thirty-fifth parallel route, perhaps the most practicable, albeit not the most politically feasible, of choices. Whipple's party included the German artist-naturalist Heinrich Baldwin Mollhausen, whom the great Prussian geographer Baron Alexander von Humboldt had sent to America.[23] Humboldt, a close friend of Bauzá who visited him in London in 1827, probably knew of the Cortés *Memorias*; he may well have mentioned the document when his young friend visited the arena of its principal focus. But whether or not the German connection brought the Cortés manuscript to Whipple's attention, his own final report of the survey, published in 1856, would include excerpts from the Cortés *Memorias* to supplement his coverage of the Indians of the region.[24]

Whipple used a translation prepared from Colonel Force's copy of the *Memorias* by Buckingham Smith, a diplomat and antiquarian who, at the time of its publication, was secretary to the American legation at Madrid. Unfortunately, Whipple published only eighteen of the most elementary paragraphs on the Apaches and scattered segments on other tribes; perhaps Smith translated no more than that. However, Whipple pointed out that valuable information lay in the remainder of the Cortés report and expressed the hope that "some individual or society will make a generous contribution to literature by publishing the report entire."

Oddly enough, that sparked no response, even though the Force copy lay handily accessible in Washington. Pioneer anthropologists, apprised of the *Memorias* by Whipple's publication, relied solely upon Smith's fragmentary and occasionally inaccurate translation, with its U.S. government imprimatur, citing that as the Cortés report. W. J. McGee's 1895 report on the Seri Indians commented appreciatively on the usefulness of the Cortés material.[25] Unhappily, Frederick Webb Hodge, annotating Indian nomenclature for Elliott Coues's 1900 edition of the Garcés diary, took a churlish view, blaming Cortés for Smith's error—not an uncommon one—in reading the manuscript capitals *J* and *F* as *T*, and sneering that "Cortés. . .seems to have cribbed most of his matter from Garcés, and bungled it in the process." Still, Hodge credited Cortés with a service of some importance in clarifying what Indians Garcés had designated as Apaches.[26] Since 1900 scholars have paid Cortés little attention, according him only such fugitive, inept references as "the Jicarillas raised crops in *joyas* or valleys not yet occupied by Spanish settlers (e.g., Cortez 1855)."[27]

In short, a valuable source has been too long neglected and abused. Cortés deserves better. So, for that matter, do Bauzá, who was instrumental in preserving the *Memorias* for posterity, and Whipple, who pointed out the importance of the whole when he published the excerpts that announced the work to pioneers of American anthropology. Notwithstanding its inevitable weaknesses and inaccuracies, this earnest essay of Cortés merits consideration whole and in the context of its time.

# NOTES

## EDITOR'S PREFACE

1. The corrected translation appears in Elizabeth A. H. John, "A Cautionary Exercise in Apache Historiography," *Journal of Arizona History* 25 (Autumn, 1984):301-15; the subsequent identification of the author of the report appears in John, "Bernardo de Gálvez on Apaches: A Cautionary Note for Gringo Historians," *Journal of Arizona History* 29 (Winter, 1988).

2. The details of Houser's life and descriptions of his work are woven throughout the copiously illustrated, interpretive analysis by Barbara H. Perlman, *Allan Houser (Ha-o-zous)* (Boston: David R. Godine, 1987).

## EDITOR'S INTRODUCTION

1. The young lieutenant's confidence may have rested in some measure upon influential connections. The 1808 roster of the Royal Corps of Engineers shows Brigadier Pedro de Cortés as subinspector, thus second in command, of the corps; if a kinsman, his benevolent interest may well have been a factor in the extraordinarily rapid advance of José María Cortés following his return to Spain. (Archivo General de Simancas [hereafter AGS], Guerra Moderna, Legajo 3794.)

2. Twenty-one of Urrutia's maps and plans survive in the British Library. They are reproduced, albeit greatly reduced, in Max L. Moorhead, *The Presidio*, 116-57.

3. *Enciclopedia Universal Illustrada Europeo-Americana*, 65: 1511. Capt. Gen. Don Josef de Urrutia appears as "Ingeniero General" on the 1800 list of officers of the Royal Corps of Engineers. AGS, Guerra Moderna, Legajo 3794.

4. The epilogue identifies an extant copy of the Cortés manuscript that Urrutia possessed.

5. The indispensable starting point for study of the Royal Corps of Engineers is Janet R. Fireman, *The Spanish Royal Corps of Engineers in the Western Borderlands, 1764-1815*, which discusses Cortés on pp. 174-85. Citations there lead directly to the personnel records of Cortés in the AGS, Guerra Moderna, Legajo 3794, and to his file in the Archivo Central Militar, in Segovia. Unless otherwise noted, all personal information on Cortés derives from those files in Spain.

6. Fireman, *Spanish Engineers*, 41.

7. The Commandancy General of the Interior Provinces, created in 1776, initially embraced all of the northernmost frontier territories of New Spain, including the Californias. When Cortés served there two decades later, the jurisdiction had narrowed to the provinces of Nueva Vizcaya, Sonora y Sinaloa, New Mexico, Texas, and Coahuila. For a concise summary of the complex evolution of the Commandancy General of the Interior Provinces from 1776 to 1824, see Thomas C. Barnes, Thomas H. Naylor, Charles W. Polzer, *Northern New Spain, A Research Guide*, 62-64.

8. Also in 1796, Cordero was appointed governor ad interim of Texas, but the appointment to the governorship of Coahuila arrived in time to forestall his depar-

ture for Texas. Cordero subsequently served as acting governor of Texas from 1805 to 1809, while retaining the governorship of Coahuila. Cordero's service record is in AGS, Guerra Moderna, Legajo 7279.

9. For an annotated translation of the manuscript copy now in the Bancroft Library, see Daniel S. Matson and Albert H. Schroeder (eds.), "Cordero's Description of the Apache – 1796," *New Mexico Historical Review* 32 (October 1957):335-56.

10. Pedro de Nava to Comandante of Janos, Chihuahua, September 11 and October 12, 1797, Janos Presidial Records, microfilm roll 14, Special Collections Library, University of Texas at El Paso.

11. Eleanor B. Adams and Fray Angélico Chávez, *The Missions of New Mexico, 1776,* xiv-xviii, provides the most complete biographical information on Domínguez. Two annotated translations of the Domínguez-Escalante diary are available: Herbert E. Bolton, *Pageant in the Wilderness: The Story of the Escalante Expedition to the Interior Basin, 1776, including the Diary and Itinerary of Father Escalante Translated and Annotated* (Salt Lake City: Utah State Historical Society, 1950); and *The Domínguez-Escalante Journal,* trans. by Fray Angélico Chávez and ed. by Ted. J. Warner (Provo: Brigham Young University Press, 1976.)

12. Bernardo de Gálvez, *Instructions for Governing the Interior Provinces of New Spain,* ed. by Donald Worcester.

13. Illuminating descriptions of the *Apaches de paz* program occur in two articles by William B. Griffen: "Apache Indians and the Northern Mexican Peace Establishments," in *Southwestern Culture History: Collected Papers in Honor of Albert H. Schroeder,* 183-95, and "The Compás: A Chiracahua Apache Family of the Late 18th and Early 19th Centuries," *The American Indian Quarterly* 7:21-48. More comprehensive treatment may be found in Griffen's book, *Apaches at War and Peace: The Janos Presidio, 1750-1758* (University of New Mexico Press, 1988).

14. *Moros de paz* were natives of Spanish North Africa who pledged themselves as vassals to the king of Spain and served as intermediaries for the Spaniards in dealing with kindred peoples. Some served as soldiers in the Spanish service, not only in the presidios of Africa, but eventually on the Iberian Peninsula as well *(Enciclopedia Universal Illustrada Europeo-Americana 36:1132).* Records concerning *Moros de paz* from 1739 through 1803 occur in AGS, Dirección General del Tesoro, Legajo 26, no. 1. The question of the influence of the successful *Moros de paz* precedent in Africa upon Spain's *Apaches de paz* experiment in New Spain deserves exploration.

15. For a brief description of that archive see Adán Benavides, Jr., "Loss by Division: The Commandancy General Archive of the Eastern Interior Provinces," *The Americas* 43(1986):203-19. The dispersal and effective loss of that archive have made it impossible to trace in any detail the activities of Lieutenant Cortés on the northern frontier.

16. Don D. Fowler, "History of Research," in *Handbook,* 1 1 *(Great Basin)*:2 2. *Handbook* vols. 8 *(California)* and 10 *(Southwest)* also attest the ethnographic importance of the Garcés and Domínguez-Escalante reports.

17. *Mapa Geogo. de la pte. de la America Sept. aumentado y corregido pr. Don José Cortés Yngo de los Rs. exercitos. Año 1799.* British Library, Add Ms. 17653c. A full-

size photograph of the map is in the Lowery Collection of the Library of Congress. See Woodbury Lowery, *The Lowery Collection*, 439.

18. Elizabeth A. H. John, "The Riddle of Mapmaker Juan Pedro Walker."

19. They were particularly concerned about inaccuracies in the *History of America* published in 1770 by Dr. William Robertson, the rector of Edinburgh and chronicler of Scotland, and deeply offended by the anti-Spanish diatribes of the Ex-Abbé Guillaume Thomas Francois Reynal in his *Histoire Philosophique et politique des établisements et du commerce des europeéns dans les deux Indes* (1774). The far-reaching deleterious impact of Reynal's work is described in Philip Wayne Powell, *Tree of Hate: Propaganda and Prejudices Affecting United States Relations with the Hispanic World* (New York: Basic Books, 1971), 108.

20. Real Academia de la Historia, Catálogo de la Colección de Don Juan Bautista Muñoz, vol. 1; *Encyclopedia Universal Illustrada Europea-Americana* 37:418.

21. Documento 75, ff. 210 et seq, Historia, tomo 301, Archivo General de la Nación (Mexico City).

22. Iris H. W. Engstrand, *Spanish Scientists in the New World*, 99.

23. "Notes and Reflections on the War with the Apache Indians in the Provinces of New Spain" is translated in Elizabeth A. H. John, "A Cautionary Exercise in Apache Historiography," *The Journal of Arizona History* 25:301-15. Subsequent research has established that the report was the work of Bernardo de Gálvez. See John, "Bernardo de Gálvez on Apaches: A Cautionary Note for Gringo Historians," *Journal of Arizona History* 29 (Winter, 1988).

24. A case in point is the September 16, 1983, address of the late Professor Enrique Tierno Galván, in his capacity as Mayor of Madrid, at his reception in the Retiro Gardens on the occasion of the 44th biennial congress of the International Statistical Institute. He articulated much the same concerns that Cortés expresses about damage done by the misleading sterotype of Spanish cruelty.

REPORT ON THE NORTHERN PROVINCES OF NEW SPAIN

1. John Wheat's translation in this volume is prepared from the earliest version yet discovered of the Cortés *Memorias*, Add. 17,562 in the Manuscripts Department of the British Library. To maximize the ethnohistorical usefulness of the work, all Indian nomenclature is presented exactly as it occurs in the document; interpretation of such terms is confined to notes. Place names, indeed all proper names, are also given as in the Cortés manuscript. The many discrepancies in names illustrate both the typical inconsistencies in eighteenth-century spelling and the changes that inevitably occur with the copying of manuscripts. *Parcialidades* is consistently translated as "groups"; the more debatable terms, "nations" and "tribes," are used only when the manuscript says *naciones* and *tribus*. The intent is to render the perception of Cortés as precisely as possible, while avoiding current controversies about appropriate terminology for the many forms of sociopolitical organization among Indian peoples.

2. Apparently the *Memorias* project was well underway in Chihuahua when the royal order of September 20, 1798, posted Cortés to Mexico City, thus forcing him to curtail his ambitious design.

3. Pacific Ocean.

4. Spaniards, following a tradition dating back to Ptolemy, set the prime meridian at Tenerife, in the Canary Islands, a judgment supported by many scientists through several centuries of heated, often nationalistic debate on the issue. Not until 1884 did the international community adopt London's Greenwich Observatory as the site of the prime meridian. (See Wilcomb E. Washburn, "The Canary Islands and the Question of the Prime Meridian: The Search for Precision in the Measurement of the Earth," *The American Neptune* 44 [spring, 1984]:77-81.)

5. La Cieneguilla was a remarkably rich, easily extracted gold deposit whose discovery in remote Sonora in February, 1771, sparked a great gold rush; other rich discoveries in the same area soon followed. (Sergio Ortega Noriega and Ignacio del Río, eds., *Historia General de Sonora* [Hermosillo, 1985], 2:278-79.) The fame of La Cieneguilla spread so swiftly that a description of the phenomenon appeared in the *History of America* that William Robertson published in 1777 in Edinburgh and Dublin.

6. Here the reference must be to the area that became the famous Santa Rita del Cobre, in the vicinity of present Silver City, New Mexico, where extensive deposits of high-grade copper extruded at the surface. Although tradition has it that Spaniards began exploiting the Santa Rita del Cobre only in 1800, the site was obviously known to Spaniards by 1785 when Capt. Antonio Cordero led an expedition pursuing Apaches into that vicinity: the diary of another officer on the same campaign mentioned El Cobre as a landmark. Lt. José Manuel Carrasco, who served under Cordero on that 1785 campaign, resigned his commission at Janos late in the eighteenth or early in the nineteenth century in order to lead the first party that worked Santa Rita del Cobre. Even if the deposit had yet to become widely known, Cortés would have had ample opportunity to hear of it in 1797 during his visits to Janos, the presidio nearest Santa Rita del Cobre, as well as through conversations with Commandant Inspector Cordero. (See Billy D. Walker, "Copper Genesis: The Early Years of Santa Rita del Cobre," *New Mexico Historical Review* 54:5-10.)

7. Approximately one-twelfth of an inch.

8. Here Cortés appears to equate San Bernardo with Espíritu Santo, which was sometimes, but not always, the case in Spanish usage. The Commandancy General grew increasingly conscious of and concerned about deficiencies in its information concerning the Texas coast, as shown in letters of Nava's successor, Commandant General Nemesio de Salcedo, to then Governor of Texas Antonio Cordero, Chihuahua, June 15 and 17, 1806. Béxar Archives, Barker Texas History Center, University of Texas at Austin.

9. The Colorado River of Texas.

10. The text reads Mazatán, but the context clearly shows that the famous harbor of Mazatlán, Sinaloa, is the reference.

11. A town that enjoys particular privileges by charter.

12. This is *pinole*, a nutritious, convenient preparation that long antedates Spanish presence in the region and remains in use in northern Mexico today, especially among the Tarahumara Indians of Chihuahua.

13. The Tlaxcalans were foremost of the Indian peoples who joined forces with conquistador Hernán Cortés, beginning in 1519, to rid themselves of Aztec

hegemony. They continued to render valuable support in subsequent Spanish expansion northward, as far as New Mexico and Texas, and were always admired as the most reliable of the Crown's Indian alles in New Spain. In 1531 Emperor Charles V rewarded the Tlaxcalans with a grant of special privileges that remained in effect to the end of Spanish dominion, jealously guarded by the Tlaxcalans and consistently upheld by the Spanish monarchy against successive challenges through the centuries. Ayer MSS. 1162 at the Newberry Library, Chicago, consists of fifteen documents demonstrating the history of the Tlaxcalan privileges from the original concession in 1531 to a decision in their favor by the government of Ferdinand VII in 1808. Marc Simmons presents a preliminary analysis of the Tlaxcalans' northernmost impact in "Tlascalans in the Spanish Borderlands," *New Mexico Historical Review* 39 (April, 1984):101-10.

14. It seems unlikely that Apaches equated Conchos and Opatas, although Cortés may have fallen into that confusion because the number of Conchos had dwindled sharply by the late eighteenth century and they were no longer conspicuous among the frontier peoples. Both Opatas and Conchos were Uto-Aztecan-speaking, *ranchería* peoples, but the more agricultural Opatas occupied river valleys of central Sonora, while Conchos lived in the Sierra Madre and eastward to the Conchos River basin. (See *Handbook* 10:337-41.)

15. The reference is to the definitive guidelines on policy toward Apaches issued by Viceroy Bernardo de Gálvez in 1786, which is discussed in the Introduction.

16. Here Cortés refers to Apaches participating in the *establecimientos de paz* that were founded under the policy decreed by Viceroy de Gálvez in 1786 (see Introduction).

17. Presumably Cortés means the first generation reared under conditions of peace, as opposed to those who entered the *establecimientos de paz* in adulthood. He probably observed at Janos that Apache youngsters were encouraged, with some success, to attend school with other youngsters of the Janos community.

18. The Introduction discusses the issue of the foreign writers whose treatment of Spain's activities in the New World had so gravely offended Spanish sensibilities.

19. For a concise description of the legal protections for Indians to which Cortés refers, see Myra Ellen Jenkins, "Spanish Colonial Policy and the Pueblo Indians," in *Southwestern Culture History: Collected Papers in Honor of Albert H. Schroeder*, Papers of the Archaeological Society of New Mexico 10:197-206.

20. The St. Lawrence River.

21. Samuel Hearne was an observant, articulate Hudson's Bay Company employee whose explorations for that company made him the first European to see the North American Arctic coast, as well as helping to quash the long-standing notion of a northwest passage. Hearne's journals, published posthumously in London in 1795 as *A Journey from the Prince of Wales's Fort in Hudson's Bay to the Northern Ocean Undertaken by Order of the Hudson's Bay Company for the Discovery of Copper Mines, a North West Passage, &c in the Years 1769, 1770, 1771, & 1772*, constitute a treasure of Canadian history and ethnography, of which the Champlain Society in Toronto twice (1911 and 1934) published informatively annotated editions. While Cortés may have seen the 1795 first edition of the Hearne journal, it is also possible that he obtained the information from the Introduction to the Report of Cook's Third Voyage, published in London in 1784. That Introduction, written by Dr. John

Douglas, the Bishop of Salisbury, who later edited Hearne's own book, included an account of Hearne's journey and the details of Hearne's route were incorporated in the general map of the world that accompanied that Cook publication.

22. Lake Winnipeg.

23. J. B. Tyrrell, the explorer who edited the Champlain Society's 1911 edition of the Hearne diary, identifies Pike Lake as probably the Whooldyah'd lake, also known as Pelican Lake, at the source of Dubawnt River.

24. Not until 1801, two years after Cortés finished his *Memorias*, were Alexander Mackenzie's journals published in London as *Voyages from Montreal on the River St. Laurence through the Continent of North America to the Frozen and Pacific Oceans in the Years 1789 and 1793.* However, Spanish officials knew of his feat soon after Mackenzie, an agent of the North West Company, reached the Pacific Coast above Vancouver Island in 1793, thus becoming the first European to cross the North American continent above present Mexico. Mackenzie's own hope was that his 1789 journal would finally demolish the myth of a northwest passage, and that his 1793 journal, which demonstrated the practicability of traversing the continent from the Atlantic to the Pacific, would stimulate a burst of British trade to exploit his overland route.

25. The Spanish and British rivalry to control Nootka Sound and Juan de Fuca Strait were key points in the contest to dominate the Pacific Northwest. Even after the ignominious withdrawal of the Spanish settlement at Nootka in 1795, that area remained a very serious concern of Spanish imperial policy. For a comprehensive analysis of that long, complex rivalry, see Warren L. Cook, *Flood Tide of Empire: Spain and the Pacific Northwest, 1543-1819* (New Haven: Yale University Press, 1973).

26. Reports were circulating among Spanish authorities that the British had established trading posts, which were by their very nature small fortifications, among the Mandan villages on the upper Missouri and possibly at other locations. (See Gayoso de Lemos to Morales, New Orleans, April 16, 1798, in A. P. Nasatir, *Before Lewis and Clark* 2:554.)

27. The reference is to the North West Company, organized in 1784 as a rival to the Hudson's Bay Company, which thrust aggressively from its Canadian base into the upper Mississippi and Missouri river basins and also into the Snake and Columbia river basins, to the great alarm of Spanish officialdom. For Spanish perception of the threat, see the report on English commerce with Indians submitted by Zenon Trudeau to the Baron de Carondelet, St. Louis, May 20, 1793, in ibid. 1:175-80.

28. British activities in the upper Mississippi and Missouri valleys in 1796 led the Spaniards to believe that a major invasion of Spanish Louisiana by British troops with thousands of Indian allies was imminent. The resulting postponement of the evacuation of Spanish posts above the thirty-first parallel east of the Mississippi River, which had been agreed in the Treaty of San Lorenzo, led to friction with the Americans, who resented the delay. (See Jack D. L. Holmes, *Gayoso: The Life of a Spanish Governor in the Mississippi Valley, 1789-1799*, 180-89.)

29. United States of America.

30. This statement on beautification and order must reflect Spanish awareness of the ambitiously planned capital city of Washington, D.C., which had been laid

out beside the Potomac River only half a dozen years before Cortés wrote his *Memorias*. Although construction was well underway toward the end of the 1790s, neither the Capitol Building nor the President's House would be far enough along for occupancy until 1800. Meanwhile, the U.S. government was headquartered in Philadelphia, which had begun as a planned city in the 1680s and may still have given that impression to Spanish envoys, although it had long since sprawled as casually as most American cities, honoring the orderly vision of founder William Penn largely in the breach.

31. Cortés apparently had access to a report of the 1790 U.S. census figure; his figure differs only slightly from that of 3,929,214 now published by the Bureau of the Census for 1790. Not so readily apparent is the basis for his 1799 estimate, which was somewhat higher than the 1800 census figure of 5,308,483. (See U.S. Bureau of the Census, *Historical Statistics of the United States: Colonial Times to 1970* [Washington, D.C.: Government Printing Office, 1975] 1:8.) However, the thirty-five percent population increase between the censuses of 1790 and 1800 certainly bore out his concern, which was further vindicated by the all-time record thirty-six percent increase between the 1800 and 1810 censuses.

32. Assuming the standard in Mexico of 2.6 miles per league, 260 miles or more.

33. Cortés is correct about the rapid accretion of three new states, but somewhat confused about their identities. The fourteenth state was Vermont, admitted in 1791; the fifteenth, Kentucky, 1792; the sixteenth, Tennessee, 1796. His false impression concerning a state of Cumberland below Kentucky, antedating that of Tennessee, derived from reports of the Cumberland Compact, by which settlers in the area of present Nashville initially established self-governance in 1780. Accounts of that development may have been garbled with later reports of the abortive state of Franklin that functioned in present eastern Tennessee from 1785 to 1790, before the United States created in 1790 the Southwest Territory that evolved into the state of Tennessee. Spanish officialdom watched the Kentucky-Tennessee region as closely as possible because its surging population of peculiarly aggressive Anglo-Americans posed an obvious threat to neighboring Spanish territories.

34. In addition to the Oneida, Onondaga, and Cayuga listed by Cortés, the Six Nations of the Iroquois Confederacy included the Mohawk, Seneca, and Tuscarora. The second Treaty of Fort Stanwix, October 22, 1784, was by no means the enduring success that Cortés assumed it to be. See Francis Paul Prucha, *The Great Father: The United States Government and the American Indians* (Lincoln: University of Nebraska Press, 1984) 1:42-45.

35. The controversial Jay's Treaty provided for Great Britain's long-overdue evacuation of its strategically important Northwest Posts, but only in return for extensive guarantees of rights and privileges that would facilitate the continued operation of Canadian fur traders south of the United States border, a condition that particularly infuriated westerners. The treaty's implications concerning both Indian relations and control of the fur trade in Upper Louisiana naturally alarmed the Spanish also. Cortés errs in thinking that the states had ratified the treaty; that responsibility belonged to the Congress and the president, who performed it in time to effect the treaty in 1796.

36. These silver pesos, the "pieces of eight" equal to eight reals, were the "Spanish dollars" copied by the United States for its own silver dollar, which was established by the Coinage Act of 1792 and first minted in 1794.

37. Also called in the United States Pinckney's Treaty, the Treaty of San Lorenzo designated the thirty-first parallel as the boundary between the territories of Spain and the United States from the Mississippi to the Atlantic, and provided for a joint boundary-survey commission to establish the line. Spain also conceded rights of navigation on the Mississippi and of deposit at New Orleans, which were essential to the economic well-being of the trans-Appalachian settlements of the United States.

38. In somewhat tardy compliance with the Treaty of San Lorenzo, the Spaniards evacuated Natchez on March 30, 1798, leaving it to the waiting American authorities.

39. Natchitoches, Louisiana, established in 1714 as the first French settlement in that colony, continued under the Spanish regime to be Louisiana's westernmost outpost and thus the key point of interaction with Texas, the easternmost province of New Spain.

40. Natchez was indeed on the American side of the thirty-first parallel. It had been in Spanish West Florida rather than in Louisiana, and was subsequently in the American Territory, now the State, of Mississippi.

41. This is the point at which Buckingham Smith began his English translation of Col. Peter Force's copy of the Cortés *Memorias*. Smith's partial translation, published in 1856 as chapter 7 of the "Report Upon the Indian Tribes" in volume 3 of the *Pacific Railway Reports*, has occasionally figured as a source in southwestern anthropological and historical studies, a matter treated in the Epilogue of the present work.

42. This list faithfully follows Lt. Col. Cordero's 1796 report on the Apaches, as does most of the information on Apaches presented by Cortés. However, Cortés omitted from his *Memorias* the Apache groups' own names for themselves as listed by Cordero, who had developed some competence in the Apache language. Listed in the same order as those of the Spanish equivalents, they are the following: Vinni ettinen-ne, Segatajen-ne, Tjuiccujen-ne, Iccujen-ne, Yntajen-ne, Sejen-ne, Cuelcajen-ne, Lipajen-ne, and Yutajen-ne. Editors Matson and Schroeder, "Cordero's Description," p. 336 n. 3, point out that the Apache call the Navajo Yutaha, which means "live far up," and that the jen-ne at the end of each name is one of various forms of tinne or dine, the word meaning people.

The younger officer, perhaps better schooled and certainly not so pressed by manifold duties and responsibilities as Commandant Inspector Cordero, extensively reorganized and elaborated Cordero's information. However, except where otherwise noted, the Cortés description of the Apaches clearly derives from the Cordero report, which is discussed in the Introduction.

43. Coyotero is now regarded as a label that was broadly applied to all Western Apaches; the Southern Tonto and Northern Tonto groups appear to have constituted major subdivisions of that broad category. For a concise exposition of contemporary understanding of the complexities of Apache tribes, bands, and clans, see Bernard L. Fontana, "Apache Indians," in *The Reader's Encyclopedia of the*

*American West*, ed. by Howard R. Lamar (New York: Thomas Y. Crowell, 1977), 34-37.

44.  Hopis. This term is more often rendered Moquis. The *g* and *q* are so close in sound and so often difficult to distinguish paleographically that it is not surprising that both spellings occur in this manuscript, an inconsistency perhaps attributable to Cortés himself, perhaps to a scribe. The inconsistent spellings are a common problem with such manuscripts.

45.  Falling into the common error of confusing the capital *T* and *F* of eighteenth-century Spanish script, Smith rendered this name as Taracones. He would subsequently render the capital *J* as *T*.

46.  The Bolsón de Mapimí is a famously forbidding, arid basin amid rugged mountains just south of the Big Bend of the Río Grande, astraddle the boundary between the Mexican states of Chihuahua (formerly in the province of Nueva Vizcaya) and Coahuila.

47.  Matson and Schroeder, editing the Cordero report, equate these terms with modern place names thus: Sevolleta as Cebolleta, north of Laguna, New Mexico; Chicoli as Chaco Canyon; Cerro-Cavezón as Cabezon, north of Cebolleta; Chusca, still current north of Gallup; Chellé as Canyon de Chelly in northeastern Arizona; Carriso in the vicinity of the Carrizo Mountains of northeastern Arizona. Tunicha is the area about the Tunicha Mountains, for which Cerro Chato may be an alternate name. Their editor, Frank D. Reeve, identifies Guadalupe as a place across the Río Puerco west of Cerro Cabezon and Agua Salada as an arroyo just north of Cebolleta.

48.  The effort to unify the Navajos under a *capitan general* selected by the nation and ratified by the governor of New Mexico dated from the treaty of friendship and alliance that Gov. Juan Bautista de Anza negotiated with Navajo emissaries in 1786. Given the complete absence of any tradition of unified leadership among the Navajos, the authority of their *capitan general* was uncertain at best, but Cordero still considered the arrangement to be functioning satisfactorily in 1796 and regarded the Navajos as faithful friends of the Spaniards, a point of view adopted by Cortés.

49.  Here Cortés differs from Cordero, who did not treat the Jicarillas separately from the Faraones, but mentioned them as a peaceful branch of the latter, living in the vicinity of Taos on the Comanche frontier. Cortés displays a much clearer grasp of the Jicarillas' history, presumably gleaned from New Mexican sources – either documents or officials – available to him at the commandancy general headquarters in Chihuahua.

50.  Picurís Pueblo, in present Taos County, New Mexico.

51.  This information derives from the diary of fathers Domínguez and Escalante, where those southern Ute divisions are reported as Muhuaches, Payuchis, Tabehuaches, and Sabuaganas. "Sogup" (for Sabuagana) appears to be an extreme example of the distortions of nomenclature that are a notorious hazard of the process of copying manuscripts. However, given that Cortés actually discussed with Father Domínguez the Indians that the old priest had visited in 1776, it is possible that Domínguez himself may have spoken of this Ute division as Sogups. Inclusion of the quite unrelated Utes in the section on Apaches seems odd. Perhaps it stems from the close alliance of some Utes in the latter eighteenth century with

the Jicarilla Apaches, then living just to the south and east of Ute territory.

52. Smith's published translation omits this entire section.

53. I.e., shamans. Cordero did not discuss this aspect of Apache religion, so Cortés clearly relies on other sources here. Some of the rhetoric may reflect the comments of Father Domínguez, who had observed many and baptized some Apaches in the preceding decade and who probably deplored in no uncertain terms whatever he had seen or heard of shamanistic practice. For current anthropological analysis of Apachean shamanism, see Morris Opler, *An Apache Life-way*, 242-67; and Opler, "The Apachean Culture Pattern and Its Origins," *Handbook* 10:372-73. Further amplification of various aspects of Apachean culture may also be found in two works of Grenville Goodwin: *Social Organization of the Western Apache* (Tucson: The University of Arizona Press, 1969) and *Western Apache Raiding and Warfare*, ed. by Keith H. Basso (Tucson: The University of Arizona Press, 1971).

54. Opler cautions in *An Apache Life-way*, p. 162, against interpreting the groom's gifts to the bride's parents as a "bride price," since they do not entitle the husband or his family to any extraordinary control over the wife or her property. On the contrary, the wife's family exercises much more stringent control over the husband than that to which the wife is subject. Moreover, the gifts are never returned, even if the woman is unfaithful or the marriage is dissolved. However, the very fact of Opler's caveat indicates that Cordero and Cortés have had ample company, well into the twentieth century, in this misapprehension.

55. This paragraph on language appears in the Smith translation. A useful summary of modern scholarship on the topic, with a brief bibliography, appears in Harry Hoijer, "The Position of the Apachean Languages in the Athapaskan Stock" in *Apachean Culture History and Ethnology*, edited by Keith H. Basso and Morris E. Opler, *Anthropological Papers of the University of Arizona* (Tucson: University of Arizona Press, 1971), no. 21:3-6.

56. The term "pueblos" is somewhat misleading here. Navajos did have places of relatively permanent residence which they occupied seasonally, and there were at least the ten recognized areas of occupation listed above in Section 1, paragraph 11. However, the clusters of Navajo homesteads in those areas did not constitute towns comparable to those of the settled Indians of New Mexico, whom the Spaniards dubbed Pueblos, or to traditional Spanish pueblos.

57. The terms given by Cortés are *la Bura, el Benado, el Berrendo, el Ozo, el Javali, el Leopardo, y Puercoespin*. We are indebted to wildlife biologists David W. Brown of the Arizona Game and Fish Department and Charles Winkler of the Texas Parks and Wildlife Department for their help in identifying the elusive *bura (Odocoileus hemionus crooki)* – desert mule deer – and in verifying translations of the other game terms. The pronghorn *(Antilocapra americana)* is often called antelope or pronghorn antelope.

58. Tuna is the fruit of the various prickly pear cacti *(Opuntia* spp.); *dátil* the fruit of the broadleafed yucca called *dátil* in Spanish and Arizona or banana yucca in English *(Yucca arizonica)*. *Pitahaya* denotes the fruit of the several columnar cacti of the Sonoran Desert: saguaro *(Carnegiea gigantea* or *Cereus gigantea);* organ pipe cactus *(Stencereus thurberi);* senita *(Lophocereus schotii);* cardón or sahuesa *(Pachycereus pringlei);* pitaya agria *(Stenocereus gummosus).* We are indebted to Dr. Bernard L. Fontana for the varieties of the giant cacti.

59. *Yucca elata*, commonly called the soap-tree yucca.

60. Useful illustrations of Apache dress appear in Alan Ferg (ed.), *Western Apache Material Culture: The Goodwin and Guenther Collections* (Tucson: University of Arizona Press, 1987).

61. It was logical that Spaniards would apply to the knee-high Apache moccasin the term *teguas* (or tewas) by which they knew the distinctive high moccasin of the Pueblos, a style that may indeed have influenced Apache footwear. *Teguas* of both Indian and Spanish manufacture figured importantly in the New Mexican export trade to the mining communities of northern New Spain, and the term came to apply throughout the region to a crudely made shoe. Although the term is generally assumed to derive from the name of the Tewa-speaking Pueblos north of Santa Fe, a distinguished scholar of the Southwest finds it to be a corruption of the seventeenth-century usage *tecoas*, apparently an Indian word of unknown origin. See Marc Simmons, "Footwear on New Mexico's Hispanic Frontier" in Lange (ed.), *Southwestern Culture History*, 224, 227.

62. This comparative comment on variations of dress and standards of neatness is unique to Cortés, although his basic description of Apache dress closely follows Cordero's report.

63. Here the Smith translation resumes.

64. Here Smith's translation breaks off again, not resuming until the section on the Comanches.

65. Little mention of trade and none of money occurs in Cordero's report. Hence this section reflects the observations and research of Cortés, though he may well have discussed these aspects with Cordero.

66. A coin worth one-eighth of a peso.

67. Again, Cortés anticipates census figures with remarkable accuracy. The census of New Mexico dated November 24, 1800, would report a population of 24,427 Spaniards and 10,557 Indians, totalling 34,984. (Spanish Archives of New Mexico [State of New Mexico Records Center], roll 14, frame 654.)

68. Here Cortés scales down Cordero's assertion that many people aged more than one hundred years take part in the hunts, but in the main he follows Cordero's report on Apache leadership and social structure.

69. Cordero draws the comparison with the ancient morris dance of the English, which the *Oxford Universal Dictionary on Historical Principles*, 3d ed., describes as "grotesque." Elements common to the Apache and morris dances include strenuous contortions and the attachment of small bells to the dancers' costumes. The name "morris" appears to derive from "morisco," meaning Moorish; the morris dance resembles such ritual dances of the Mediterranean as the moriscos, matachines, and Moors' and Christians' dances that spread to Hispanic America, even as far north as New Mexico. (*The New Encyclopedia Britannica*, 15th ed.) Hence it is intriguing that Cordero noted the similarity to the English ritual dance rather than those common to Iberia.

70. Here Cortés, following Cordero, refers to the masked dancers whose impersonation of the supernatural Mountain Spirits figured importantly in certain Chiricahua rituals. For detailed treatment of the topic, consult Opler, *An Apache Life-way*.

71. The question of a taboo on fish is discussed in Opler, *An Apache Life-way*, 330-32.

72. Cortés gives fuller detail than Cordero on the stylistic variations among in-

digenous Apache weapons. After substantially contradicting Cordero's brief comment of 1796 on the subject of firearms among the Apaches, he gives his own extended analysis of the practical and political issues involved.

73. Here Cortés reviews the longstanding, albeit virtually dead, issue of restrictions upon gifts and sales of guns and ammunition to Indians. The evolution of Spanish policy on that subject, which by 1799 routinely entailed supplying guns and ammunition to all of the Indian allies in the Interior Provinces, is traced in Elizabeth A. H. John, *Storms Brewed in Other Men's Worlds*.

74. *Droga* presumably refers to the various alcoholic beverages—rum, brandy, whiskey, etc.—which were staples in the British, American, and, earlier, the French trade with all Indians.

75. Although gun repair did pose a problem for Indians, that lack was hardly "total." Many had access to repair services in the Spanish settlements that they frequented and sometimes in certain Indian villages. Gun repair was among the most popular services provided to Indian visitors, either by gift or by barter, at such settlements as Santa Fe in New Mexico and San Antonio and Nacogdoches in Texas. Records of itinerant blacksmiths plying their trade sporadically at the Taovayas village on Red River date back at least to the unlawful sojourn there of French smith Pedro Vial in the 1780s; it is not improbable that other such itinerant smiths worked from time to time in Plains Indian villages farther northward.

76. The vendetta acutally dates back to the early eighteenth century, when newly equestrian Comanches descended from the northern Rockies and leagued with Utes to oust Apaches from the central plains, shattering the eastern Apachería and driving such groups as the Jicarillas and the Lipanes to seek refuge in alliance with the Spaniards of New Mexico and Texas respectively. While control of the buffalo ranges was surely a major factor, so was raiding for horses, and casualties in the contest quickly spawned imperatives of vengeance on all sides, thus perpetuating bitter enmities that appeared to date from time immemorial. See John, *Storms Brewed in Other Men's Worlds*, 245 et seq.

77. None of the material in this section appears in Cordero's report.

78. Credulity is strained by the apparent statement that the group lay face down in the riverbed for three days. However, on closer reading, it appears that the three days refers to the entire time spent in the post-fire ritual: the retrieval and burial of the bones and removal to the new location occurred on the first day after the cremation; on the second day they threw themselves face down into the sand; the third day was the time of their arising. So they would not have sustained that posture for more than twenty-four hours, and possibly much less if they lay down late on the second day and arose early on the third. Even that interpretation leaves ample cause for astonishment.

79. The episode was little more puzzling and intriguing to Cortés and the old hands at Janos than to today's scholars of the Apaches, three of whom have kindly read this translation and offered comments. Dr. Morris E. Opler points out that some of the elements are fairly standard Apache practice: the removal of the dying person from his home; the destruction of a home associated with a death and of the property of the deceased; the move of the local group from the death site. Other elements are quite extraordinary: the burning of the body before final disposal of the remains (as opposed to the customary immediate burial of the corpse); the contact

with the remains after cremation; the participation of so many people, including women, in the death and burial procedures; the destruction of all the homes of the group, the generous use of fire, the "fence" of arrows and lances. One possible explanation is that the dying man was reputed to be a witch, who used his supernatural power to harm rather than to benefit his fellows. Fire is considered the most powerful weapon that can be used against witches or objects of witchcraft, but arrows and pointed objects also were used to combat witchcraft. (Since the witch used invisible magical arrows with which to "shoot" his victims, others tried to confound him by using real arrows against him.) The extensive use of fire seems to Opler to suggest that either witchcraft or something else very much dreaded was involved. The participation of the mother-in-law in the death watch and cremation is particularly puzzling in view of the Apaches' absolute rule of avoidance in that relationship. (Summarized from personal communications of Opler to John, October 3 and November 2, 1984, and January 3, 1985.)

Dr. William B. Griffen and Dr. Henry F. Dobyns each raised the interesting possibility that the Indians observed by Cortés at Janos were not altogether typical Apaches as he assumed, but included elements of the earlier indigenes of that area–e.g., the Janos, Jócomes, Sumas–who faded away early in the eighteenth century and whose remnants may have been absorbed by the conquering Apaches. Cremation is thought to have been practiced by those peoples and might have persisted among their descendants. (Griffen to John, September 7, 1984, and Dobyns to John, April 30, 1985.)

Dobyns also raises the possibility that the extensive burning was a response to fear of an infectious disease such as smallpox or measles. However, the fact that the group did not move far away seems to negate that speculation: by the latter eighteenth century Apaches were keenly aware of the dangers of contagion and were quick to flee afflicted settlements for the safety of remote mountains until the epidemic subsided.

80. "Caribes" is a term applied to the Indians of the Antilles and the adjacent continent at the time of discovery. It acquired an extended meaning of cannibal, man-eater, or savage.

81. Here the Smith translation resumes, continuing through paragraphs 2, 3, and 4 on the Comanches.

82. Here Cortés is a bit confused. The major divisions of the Comanche nation were the Cuchanticas (sometimes rendered as Cuchanecs), the Yamparicas, and the Jupes, each comprised of many bands. Rapidly expanding their range at the expense of eastern Apaches, by the latter eighteenth century they fell into two broad geographic categories: the *Orientales* (easterners), neighboring Texas, and the *Occidentales* (westerners), neighboring New Mexico. Most Orientales were Cuchanecs, but ever-growing numbers of Yamparicas moved southeastward to enjoy the richer, milder buffalo ranges toward Texas. Most Yamparicas and Jupes and some Cuchanticas were *Occidentales*.

83. Here Cortés refers to the political and economic relationship that began with the treaties of peace and alliance that the Comanches *Occidentales* celebrated with the Spaniards at Pecos in February, 1786, and the analogous treaty of the *Orientales* at San Antonio in October, 1785. For development of that alliance, see John, *Storms Brewed in Other Men's Worlds*, 664-716.

84. It is surprising that Cortés is unaware of the longstanding Comanche alliances with the Wichitan villagers of the Red and Brazos river basins and their occasional cooperation with other Indian peoples on the northern frontier of Texas. These connections figured importantly in Spanish management of Indian affairs in that province.

85. Now generally spelled Tawakoni, this is one of the four Wichitan groups that figured importantly on the northern frontier of Texas from the mid-eighteenth century onward. (See John, *Storms Brewed in Other Men's Worlds*, 304-306, 338-42 pass.). Such sources as the reports of Athanase de Mézières and Fray Juan Agustín Morfi, which were available to Cortés in the archive of the commandancy general at Chihuahua, report two Tawakoni villages on the Brazos, some twenty miles apart, and of course give higher population figures for the Tawakonis. Morfi had relied heavily upon the firsthand reports of de Mézières, and it is obvious that Cortés drew to some extent on both. The basis for his many deviations from those two sources is not apparent; perhaps he plucked data somewhat randomly from later, less comprehensive reports.

86. *Parcialidades del Norte* is the term used by Cortés, meaning the peoples commonly called Norteños or Nations of the North. His presumption of linguistic homogeneity among all Norteños was quite wrong.

87. These names, now usually written as Tonkawas, Yojuanes, and Mayeyes, denote the three best known of the Tonkawan-speaking groups that had ranged along the lower Brazos and Trinity basins from time immemorial. As their numbers dwindled under the pressures of eighteenth-century events, they coalesced as Tonkawas.

88. This description of the Tonkawas obviously derives from the direct observations that de Mézières reported to Commandant Gen. Teodoro de Croix, September 2, 1779. See Herbert E. Bolton, *Athanase de Mézières and the Louisiana-Texas Frontier, 1768-1780* 2:278-79.

89. This name, now generally written as Taovayas, fell into disuse by the mid-nineteenth century, although in the eighteenth century the Taovayas were more numerous and powerful than the Wichitas, under whose name all of the Wichitan bands coalesced in the twentieth century. From about 1757 to 1812, their village and that of the Wichitas, and sometimes that of the Iscanis also, occupied a strategic location astride the Red River, just west of the Cross Timbers in present Montague County, Texas, and Jefferson County, Oklahoma. Cortés relied upon the description written by de Mézières, who visited the Taovayas in 1778, two decades before Cortés wrote his *Memorias*. A decade after Cortés, an Anglo-American visitor wrote a more detailed account of those villages, with much of the kind of ethnographic detail that so fascinated Cortés. See Bolton, *Athanase de Mézières* 2:201-204; Elizabeth A. H. John, "Portrait of A Wichita Village, 1808," *The Chronicles of Oklahoma* 60 (Winter, 1982-83):412-37.

90. *Ceparaciones* (correctly *separaciones*) apparently refers to the arbors and storage platforms that supplemented Wichitan dwellings.

91. In Mexico, approximately 2.6 bushels.

92. Wichitan women wove mats from long strips of squashes and pumpkins, which they dried, creating an efficient trail food for themselves and a popular item in their trade with such nomads as the Comanches.

93. De Mézières, reporting the abundance of excellent fish available in the Red

River, noted that the Taovayas did not care for them, an accurate reflection of the widespread fish taboo among Indians of the Plains and the Southwest, including the Wichitan peoples. It is puzzling that Cortés ignored that information, even though he reported the less firmly established aversion to fish among Apaches.

94. The Western, or Upper, Cross Timbers was one of two long, narrow bands of dense timber running northward from the Brazos River basin to the Canadian River between the ninety-sixth and ninety-ninth meridians. Travelers venturing north from San Antonio or the Tawakoni villages on the Brazos often followed the edge of the Cross Timbers as a handy guide to the Taovayas villages. In addition to the fuel and timber for construction noted by de Mézières, the Cross Timbers were rich in a considerable array of fruits and nuts that Wichita women and children gathered and stored, greatly enriching the subsistence of their people.

95. Presumably the Taovayas envisioned mountain lions or other wildcats indigenous to the Plains environment.

96. This account of the Wichitas derives from de Mézières' report of his visit to their village on the upper Brazos in 1772 (Bolton, *Athanase de Mézières* 1:294-97). Ordinarily the Wichitas lived in close proximity to the Taovayas, but in the early 1770s severe pressure from Osage raiders drove both the Wichitas and the Taovayas to flee temporarily the excellent location on the Red River that Cortés describes above. While the Taovayas established themselves farther up the Red River, the Wichitas resorted to a singularly arid, treeless locale that permitted neither their traditional agriculture nor their customary construction of grass houses, but did offer them handy proximity to rich buffalo ranges and to their Comanche trading partners as well as safer distance from the Osages. De Mézières summoned the Taovayas to meet him at the Wichita village and urged both groups to join forces again in a more suitable location. They agreed, and by 1778 resumed their former location on Red River, where they remained until another surge of Osage raids drove them away in the early nineteenth century.

97. Now usually spelled as Akokisas and Bidais, the first and second of these groups were the westernmost of the Atakapan-speaking peoples, and were indeed reported by de Mézières as kindred groups. The Akokisas were strictly hunters and gatherers; the Bidais practiced some agriculture. Both were much less advanced culturally than the settled Caddo villagers just to the north of them. Texas (or Tejas), derived from the Caddo term *Tayshas* (allies or friends), was the name by which Spaniards first knew collectively the western Caddo peoples, or Hasinai, who had lived in present northeastern Texas from time immemorial. (See nn. 100 and 101, below.) In 1778 de Mézières reported the Texas to be divided into various bands, known under the names Azinays, Nevadizoes, Nadacogs, and Nacogdoches, but Cortés obviously did not grasp those connections and distinctions.

98. Presidio San Agustín de Ahumada was established in 1756 on the left bank of the Trinity River, not far above Trinity Bay, among the Akokisas Indians, after whom the enterprise was informally called *El Orcoquisac*. Mission Nuestra Señora de la Luz was established nearby but it never thrived, nor did the projected civil settlement ever materialize. The whole effort was abandonned actually in 1771 and officially in 1773. (See John, *Storms Brewed in Other Men's Worlds*, 347-48, 435-38, 448.)

99. Here Cortés falls into some confusion about the Wichitan groups. Flechazo

denotes the second of the Tawakoni villages visited by de Mézières in 1772 and 1779, named for the founding chief, El Flechazo.

The kindred Yscanis, now usually spelled Iscanis, were another Wichitan group, the most elusive and occasionally scattered of the four. They were sometimes reported living adjacent to the Taovayas and Wichitas on Red River, at other times near the Tawakonis on the Brazos, and occasionally in the Trinity basin nearer the Kichais. Clearly Cortés failed to grasp their connection with the other Wichitan groups that he discussed, although de Mézières reported it.

The Quitseis, now spelled Kichais, were almost identical in culture to the Wichitan peoples, but were a linguistically separate Caddoan-speaking village people, few in number, and the most consistently peaceful of all the Norteños towards the Spaniards. De Mézières, who visited them in 1772, reported their cultural similarity and customary alliance with the four Wichitan groups and also their close friendship with the neighboring eastern and western Caddo groups. (Bolton, *Athanase de Mézières* 1:285-86.)

100. Here again Cortés falls into difficulty with the nomenclature of the Hasinais, or Texas, Caddo-speaking villagers of the Trinity and Sabine river basins. It is clear that he refers to the Nebedaches, Ais, and Nasonis. Very possibly Saisesdemolida is a distortion of the 1779 de Mézières report of the near extinction of the village of the Ais (Bolton, *Athanase de Mézières* 1:257). Nahuchichos and Ynamiches must also be garbles of Caddo village names, since the area described was the homeland of that nation.

101. Here Cortés compounds confusion. The Nadacos (today spelled Anadarkos) and Nacogdoches were western Caddo peoples of the Hasinais or Texas category discussed above. The Kichais were mentioned two paragraphs earlier under the variant spelling Quitseis. The Wichitas and Taovayas were treated four and five paragraphs earlier, under the variant spellings "Obedsitas" and "Taobayaces."

102. The eighteen nations are those named after the discussion of the Taboayaces (Taovayas), beginning with the Obedsitas (Wichitas); of course, the number dwindles with subtraction of the variant duplications. While the customs of all the village peoples did resemble in many respects those reported for the Taovayas and Tawakonis, the totally nomadic culture of the Tonkawas differed so entirely from that of the Wichitan villagers as to make nonsense of this statement by Cortés. There was in fact a wide gamut of cultures among the Indians whom Cortés jumbled together so oddly here. In his haste to finish this report before undertaking his new assignment, Cortés may simply have despaired of sorting out the reports from Texas.

103. Annual presents from the Crown, patterned on longstanding French practice in neighboring Louisiana, were crucial components of the treaties of friendship and alliance that Spain contracted with most Indian peoples in Texas from the 1770s onward. Occasional visits of British and Anglo-American traders to Indians on the northern Texas frontier, particularly the Taovayas and Wichita villages on Red River, became a matter of concern in the 1770s; by the 1790s the traffic was increasing so rapidly as to constitute a serious threat to the well-being of Spanish Texas.

104. *Naciones Caribes* is the term used by Cortés. It may reflect the belief that the coastal groups of Texas belonged to the Carib peoples whom the Spaniards had encountered in the West Indies, a belief still entertained by some students of linguistics. (*Handbook* 10:362). On the other hand, Cortés may intend the meaning, "cruel, inhuman person" or "cannibal," which the term *caribe* came to have in the Spanish language.

105. Here Cortés deals with the welter of small coastal groups whose identification and classification still hold challenges for scholars. (For the most current analyses, see T. N. Campbell, "Coahuiltecans and Their Neighbors," and W. W. Newcomb, Jr., "Karankawa," in *Handbook*, 10:343-58 and 359-67.) The first five, now usually written as Karankawas, Cocos, Cujanes, Copanos, and Coapites, were Karankawan-speaking groups who inhabited the central Texas coastal region. The last, now usually written as Aranamas, ranged the coastal plain between the San Antonio and Guadalupe rivers and appear to have been Coahuiltecan speakers.

106. The establishments to which Cortés refers were Mission Nuestra Señora del Espíritu Santo, originally established on the coast in 1722 for Karankawa groups who rejected it, then moved inland to serve Aranamas on the Guadalupe River in 1726, and finally, still serving Aranamas, moved to the San Antonio River, at present Goliad, Texas, in 1749. Mission Nuestra Señora del Rosario was established five miles upstream from Mission Espíritu Santo in 1754, in another effort to serve the Karankawas, Cujanes, Coapites, and Copanos. Although neither of the two Goliad missions thrived, and apostates from those establishments constituted a serious problem upon which de Mézières wrote repeatedly in the 1770s, both enterprises endured until secularization in 1830 and 1831. A final effort to meet the Karankawas on their own ground was Mission Nuestra Señora del Refugio, established on the coast in the early 1790s. The surprising extent of its eventual success could not have been known to Cortés, but Mission Refugio also endured until secularization in 1830. While those were indeed extraordinarily troubled missions, they were not such total failures as Cortés assumed.

107. Here Cortés conveys the stereotype of the ferocious cannibal Karankawas that continues to stalk those ill-starred coastal people even in extinction. Anthropologist W. W. Newcomb, Jr., points out that there is little to substantiate their reputation for routinely consuming human flesh as food, and indeed some evidence to the contrary, although the Karankawan peoples undoubtedly shared the widespread custom of ritual cannibalism for purposes of revenge and of religious belief, as did the neighboring Atakapan, Caddoan, Wichitan, and Tonkawan peoples (Newcomb, *Handbook* 10:366).

108. The succeeding paragraphs follow very closely the information given in a letter from Louisiana's Governor-General Estevan Miró to Commandant Gen. Josef Antonio Rengel, dated New Orleans, December 12, 1785. Rengel's predecessor as commandant general of the Interior Provinces, Felipe de Neve, had written in December, 1783, requesting any information available in the archives of New Orleans that might acquaint the commandancy general with the Indian nations bordering on the Interior Provinces, in order to facilitate management of Indian affairs. He also requested a map to aid his understanding. Unfortunately, the French had left no such map when they relinquished Louisiana in 1765, and the Spaniards

had yet to develop one. But Miró's response represents a considerable and very useful effort to accommodate the commandant general of the neighboring jurisdiction. Naturally, Cortés found it available in the archive of the commandancy general at Chihuahua. Except where otherwise noted, this section derives from the Miró report, which was in turn compiled from many reports of travelers and hunters. Miró's letter appears in translation in two collections of documents: Lawrence Kinnaird, ed., *Spain in the Mississippi Valley, 1765-1794* 2:159-67, and A. P. Nasatir, ed., *Before Lewis and Clark* 1:119-27.

109. Here Cortés encounters the eastern Caddo peoples, whose territory from time immemorial had lain principally in present northwestern Louisiana: the prestigious Kadohadachos, Great and Little, who were considered the "true" ancestral Caddo stock; the Yatasis; the Natchitoches, among whom the French founded the oldest and westernmost settlement in present Louisiana; and the Adaes, whose name figures importantly in early Texas history. (Presidio Los Adaes, established in 1722 at the Adaes village, near present Robeline, Louisiana, was the capital of Spanish Texas from 1722 to 1769.)

Rapides may be an alternative name for the Avoyel, a small indigenous tribe living on the lower Red River just below the Rapides, a famous geographic point of reference on that stream. The rest of the list represents only some of the many groups, mostly quite small, that emigrated westward across the Mississippi into Spanish Louisiana after the Treaty of Paris of 1763 turned their homelands in Spanish Florida over to British dominion. Many preferred to take their chances with the Spanish Crown in Louisiana; some would make that choice again after 1803, moving on to Spanish Texas after the Louisiana Purchase subjected them to American rule. The most numerous and now the best known of those migrants were the frequently allied Alibamones and Chatos (now known as Alabamas and Coushattas), both of whom were Creek, or Muskogee, peoples. The Pacanas were another of the Muskogee peoples who moved to Red River in the 1760s from their aboriginal homeland in present Alabama. They emigrated and settled along with the Apalaches, which suggests that Ochonias may be a garbling of Osochi, a term that Swanton found in a Spanish map of 1765 as an alternative to Apalache, and that the people listed by Miró as Ochonias were the group usually known as Apalaches.

The Biloxis were a Siouan tribe thought to have emigrated very early from the Ohio Valley to the coastal region that became Spanish Florida, and subsequently joined in the emigration to Red River after the 1760s transfer of their homeland to British dominion. Editorial speculation on the identities of the Rapides and Ochonias is based upon information in John R. Swanton, *The Indians of the Southeastern United States*, together with extensive reading of late eighteenth- and early nineteenth-century reports on Indians of the Red River basin.

110. Better known historically as the Arkansas Post, this strategic post, founded by Henri de Tonti in 1682, endured throughout the French and Spanish regimes in Louisiana. After the Louisiana Purchase, the U.S. government stationed a small garrison at the Arkansas Post, renaming it Fort Madison, and also operated a factory (government trading post for Indians) there from 1805 to 1810.

111. The Arkansas Indians, better known in the American period as Quapaws, were among the Dhegiha Sioux peoples—Omahas, Osages, Kansas, and

Poncas–who appear to have emigrated westward and southwestward from the Ohio valley some years before Europeans first observed them in the latter seventeenth century. Initially found in four large villages on the Mississippi, with an estimated strength of six thousand to fifteen thousand, the Quapaws proved so vulnerable to epidemic diseases and alcohol that by 1763 they had dwindled to seven hundred, divided among the three villages on the Arkansas River near the Arkansas Post. The initial four villages were called Kappa, Osotouy, Tourima and Tongigua, but by 1700 attrition from epidemics was so great that the people of Tourima joined with those of Kappa, and soon afterward those of Tongigua consolidated with "New Kappa," leaving only two villages (David Baird, *The Quapaw Indians*, 3, 10, 27, 37). Although by the end of the eighteenth century their population had dwindled still further, to less than six hundred, the Quapaws again had three villages, whose names John Sibley reported in 1805 as Ocapas, Ousolu, and Tawanima (John Sibley, "Historical Sketches of the Indian tribes in Louisiana," 725.) The first two obviously correlate with the first two listed by Cortés. The third suggests that the Tourimas had again asserted a separate identity.

112. This must have been, as Carl Chapman suggests, just a hunting camp of the Little Osages, whose permanent village was then on the Osage River, as Cortés notes in Section 3, paragraph 27 (Chapman, *Origin of the Osage Indian Tribe*, 85).

113. Ste. Geneviève and St. Louis, in present Missouri.

114. These names are now most often written as Sioux, Big Osages, Iowas, Kansas, Skidi Pawnees, Sauks, Otos (represented here by both Autodatas and Hotós), Little Osages, Missouris, Fox, and Kaskaskias. For the reader's convenience, these identifications will be repeated below at the paragraphs describing each group.

115. This reference to English activity on the upper Missouri does not appear in the Miró report; hence it originates with Cortés.

116. Now ordinarily written as Arikara.

117. The Great Falls of the Missouri River.

118. "This part" presumably refers to the upper reaches of the Missouri now under discussion; the mountains, of course, are the Rockies. Miró speaks of the chain of mountains that start just east of Santa Fe and reportedly go to the province of Quivira, but Cortés was much too skeptical about the persistent myth of Quivira to include that reference in his own version. Indeed, Miró's naive reference to Quivira must have helped to provoke Cortés to end his *Memorias* with such an emphatic repudiation of the Quivira myth.

119. It seems odd that Cortés copied without criticizing this misconception of the Miró report. Having studied the journal of the travels in the Colorado River basin of Father Garcés, and also that of fathers Domínguez and Escalante, he was certainly as well aware of that major river system flowing to the Gulf of California as of the Río Grande system mentioned here; indeed, the map that Cortés prepared to accompany the *Memorias* clearly displays that knowledge.

120. Cortés writes *al Oeste ¼ Noroest*.

121. Cortés inserted these last two sentences of caveat about the speculative nature of ideas about the terrain beyond the Great Falls of the Missouri instead of including the Miró report's assertions that the river "should flow as far as the other chain of mountains which passes between the Colorado River and the province of

Teguayo" (i.e., the land of the Tewa-speaking Pueblos of the upper Río Grande valley), and that "the rivers to the east of this mountain, to the north of Teguayo, must empty into the Missouri, which, as it seems, has its source here, because to the west of these mountains, the sea or the Bay of the West almost washes their base."

122. This island, opposite the small creek now called Coldwater, was the campsite of the Lewis and Clark expedition on May 14, 1804, the first night of their long trek to the Pacific. See Elliott Coues, ed., *History of the Expedition of Lewis and Clark* 1:5.

123. Although Cortés uses *aldea* in its usual meaning (village or hamlet) elsewhere in the *Memorias,* that is not appropriate here. The Sioux never lived that far south, nor does the context suggest that any such occupation ever occurred. The Bancroft Library's manuscript of the Miró report, from which both Kinnaird and Nasatir worked, gives instead the long-established place name, "portage des los Suis." That commemorates an early incident of Indian warfare, when Sioux raiders coming down the Mississippi carried their canoes across that narrow tongue of land to the Missouri River in order to surprise some Missouri Indian defenders who had expected to confront the invading Sioux at the junction of the Mississippi and Missouri rivers. The strategic importance of the location was well understood by the French and by the Spaniards, who established the village of Portage des Sioux there in 1799 – the very year of the Cortés *Memorias* – to offset a possible American fortification on the opposite side of the Mississippi (Louis Houck, *A History of Missouri,* 2:87-90.) Finding the French *portage* transformed into the *aldea* of such different import, either in the creation at New Orleans of the copy that Miró sent to Chihuahua or by an unaccountable blunder of the scholarly Cortés or a subsequent copyist, provides yet another cautionary example of the garbling that so easily mars the integrity of manuscripts.

124. This coal bank directly on the right shore of the Missouri, about twelve miles above its confluence with the Mississippi, was called La Charbonnière by early settlers of the region (Alphonse Wetmore, *Gazetteer of the State of Missouri* [St. Louis, 1837], 248).

125. According to Coues, *Lewis and Clark* 1:9 n. 11, the French name of the stream was Loutre; the Americans would call it Otter Creek.

126. The Gasconade River.

127. The Meramec River.

128. The Osage River.

129. The Niangua River.

130. The Bancroft Library copy reports ninety-eight islands rather than the eighty-nine given by Cortés, another example of the discrepancies that creep in as manuscripts are copied.

131. Cedar River.

132. In Spain, the *braza* measured 1.7 meters, or 1.8 yards.

133. Lamine River.

134. The Big and Little Chariton rivers.

135. The Des Moines River.

136. The Grand River.

137. The Kansas River.

138. The wording here is a bit confusing: Cortés says *la Republica de los Panis*, while the Bancroft manuscript says *"la Republica, o Panis"*. However, the reference is clearly to the band of Pawnees who became known as Republican by the latter eighteenth century.

139. The Nishnabotna River.

140. Weeping Water Creek.

141. The Platte River.

142. The Otos.

143. Cortés adopted the French term "Panis" without noting that in New Mexico the same people were known as "Pananas"; it would be interesting to know whether he grasped the connection.

144. Eventually known to Americans as the Skidi Pawnees, this band of the Pawnees were known to the Spaniards of Texas as Aguages and to those of New Mexico as Aas.

145. The Sioux River.

146. This is a copyist's error for *calumetes;* the word appears correctly in the Bancroft manuscript. Calumets were the ornamented ceremonial pipes for which the Indians made bowls of catlinite, the unique soft red stone named for the painter George Catlin.

147. The Niobrara River.

148. Again, the term given is "O ¼ N.O."

149. Pados appears to be an echo of the early eighteenth-century presence of the Comanches, then known to the French as Paducas or Pados. That echo also occurs as Pados in Jean Baptiste Truteau's "Description of the Upper Missouri," written in 1796 (Nasatir, *Before Lewis and Clark*, 2: 379), and repeatedly as Padouca in William Clark's journal of his great expedition and related correspondence. Neither Cortés, who knew the Comanches as the dominant nation roving the lands between New Mexico and Texas, nor Clark had any basis for recognizing the connection between the Comanches who were so prominent southward in the late eighteenth century and the Pados whose disappearance from the northern plains gave rise to so much speculation.

150. Perhaps Toquibacos is an old Comanche band name, but it seems more likely to indicate a band of one of the other nations—e.g., Kiowa or Arapaho—who roved the upper Missouri basin in the latter eighteenth century and may indeed have found it necessary to build some small stockades for protection against increasingly dangerous incursions by better-armed, more numerous Sioux raiders.

151. *Cabras* is the term in the manuscript. Donald Jackson (ed.) in *Letters of the Lewis and Clark Expedition* 1:225 n. 3, notes that the term *cabree,* derived from the French *cabril* and the Spanish *cabras* for goat, became an Americanism for the pronghorn, beginning with the reports of Lewis and Clark.

152. *Gamos* is the term in the manuscript, listed as distinct from *benados* (deer). In contemporary Spanish the term denotes the buck of the fallow deer, an impressively antlered Eurasian species, obviously not applicable here. It seems logical that Spaniards applied *gamo* to the large, also impressively antlered wapiti, commonly called elk, whose abundance made them important in the diet and the trade of the region discussed here.

153. Since the pheasant is an Old World bird that was not introduced into this

region until the latter nineteenth century, the report may refer to the indigenous grouse, quail, or partridge.

154. The Big Osages.

155. The Little Osages.

156. Laytanes, or Hietans, was a term often applied to Comanches. If, as the punctuation suggests, Cortés believed the term to denote Apaches, he was misled. Kinnaird's translation of Miró displays the same punctuation, as does the Bancroft manuscript. That of Nasatir omits the commas, indicating that the horses were obtained either from Comanches or from Apaches. But the nations of the Missouri had not had access for many decades to Apaches, other than the small group of Catakas, or Kiowa Apaches, who fled northward when the eastern Apachería dispersed under Comanche and Ute pressure early in the eighteenth century. (See John, "An Earlier Chapter of Kiowa History," 381-83.) Hence it seems much more likely that the nations of the Missouri were relying upon Comanches and not Apaches for horses in the latter eighteenth century.

157. *Gatos monteses* is the term given by Cortés.

158. The specific boundaries given for the hunting grounds of each of the groups provide an interesting refutation of the self-serving assumption of many Anglo-Americans that Indians had no well-defined sense of property.

159. The Missouris.

160. *Prado de fuego* is the term in the manuscript. William Clark, who noted the potential usefulness of the Fire Prairie site on his way up the Missouri in 1804, selected it in 1808 as the locale for the first factory established by the U.S. government particularly for the Osage Indians. Accordingly, factor George C. Sibley established Fort Osage on a bluff three miles above Fire Prairie in the fall of 1808 (George C. Sibley, Diary II, entries for 1808. Lindenwood Collection, Missouri Historical Society, St. Louis).

161. The Kansas, also known as Kaws.

162. The Nemaha River.

163. The Otos.

164. The Iowas.

165. In this paragraph Cortés deviates from the Miró report, supplying instead the more current information available to him in 1799. Kinnaird renders the Miró paragraph as follows: "Whenever the Otos are at war with the Sioux, they prefer to trade with Ylinoa, and it is always to be feared that the English may enter into the villages of the Pawnees and the Otos as they did in 1773 and 1777. The extent of the hunting grounds of the Otos is from the great Nemaha River up to the Boyer River."

166. The Pawnees. Here Cortés returns to the Miró text.

167. Presumably the Republican River.

168. The Skidi Pawnees.

169. The Loup River.

170. The Arikaras were often called "Rees" in the American period. Miró gave an estimate of nine hundred warriors rather than one thousand.

171. Although Pados, or Padoucas, is generally equated with Comanches (as

noted with Section 3, paragraph 22, above), this reference seems more likely to indicate remnants of Apache groups that dispersed northwards when Comanches and Utes shattered the Apachería of the central plains early in the eighteenth century. The only survivors of those groups presently known are the group that found refuge in the Kiowa camp circle, hence becoming known historically as the Kiowa Apaches.

172. Another confusion of the nomenclature of Comanches–often called Laytanes–and Apaches. This paragraph clearly describes the Comanche situation of the latter eighteenth century, when some Comanche bands still lived in the Rocky Mountains of present Colorado while others were migrating southward from the Arkansas to the Red, the Brazos, and even the Colorado river basins of Texas.

173. The Sioux, of whose complex diversity Miró's sources apparently gave little inkling, although the analogy to the Comanches is quite apt.

174. *Higados-duros* translates literally as hard-livers. Clearly the reference is to the Hidatsas and Mandans, whose villages were an important hub of commerce on the northern plains.

175. Here ends the reliance of Cortés upon the Miró report. The latter concludes with this caveat: "There may be some difference in the names of the Indian tribes and the rivers, but I give those which are known by the French who have been the masters of this province." Nasatir believes this to be an insertion added after the initial composition of the unsigned draft that is now in the Bancroft Library.

176. Here again resumes the Buckingham Smith translation published in the Pacific Railway Survey report; now it continues uninterrupted to the end of the *Memorias.*

177. During the Pueblo Revolt of 1680 the Hopis forcibly rid themselves of Spanish presence in their villages in present northern Arizona. Although the Hopis of Awatovi briefly welcomed Franciscans back to their village in 1700 and even agreed to permit a new mission there, the dominant Hopi leadership resolved never to permit any reestablishment of Spaniards in their world, and swiftly extirpated nonconforming Awatovi to ensure that purpose. The Hopis successfully rebuffed all subsequent efforts of the Spaniards to resume any activities–religious, military, or political–among them.

178. Here Cortés follows the Domínguez-Escalante diary, which gives the names as Oraybi, Tanos, Mossonganabi, Xipaolabi, Xongopabi, and Gualpis (Bolton, *Pageant in the Wilderness,* 232-35). Today those names are ordinarily spelled as Oraibi, Hano, Mishongnovi, Shipaulovi, Shongopavi, and Walpi. Hano (also known as Tewa Village), a community of Tewa speakers who have lived with the Hopi of First Mesa for some three centuries, originated with the surge of Tewa-speaking Pueblos who fled from the upper Rio Grande to the Hopis for refuge from the turmoils of the latter seventeenth century. The seventh, reported here as unnamed, must have been Sichomovi (*Handbook,* 10:550-52, 587).

179. For the details in paragraphs 2, 3, and 4, Cortés appears to rely principally upon the descriptions in the diary of Fray Francisco Garcés, who visited the Hopi villages in 1776. (See Coues, *On the Trail of a Spanish Pioneer* 2:361-63, 382-85.)

However, it should be remembered that Cortés also availed himself of the oral recollections of Fray Domínguez, as well as studying the Domínguez-Escalante diary.

180. Roughly four and a half feet, assuming the *vara* at about thirty-three inches.

181. The term used is *color mas abierto*.

182. For a well-illustrated description of such musical instruments, see Laurinda Queen, "Southwestern Indian Musical Instruments," *The Smoke Signal*, no 35 (Tucson: Tucson Corral of the Westerners, Spring, 1978).

183. This section of the *Memorias*, as translated by Buckingham Smith and presented in the Railway Survey Report, was considered by anthropologist W. J. McGee to be "among the more useful contemporary records" of the Seri. Specifically, he found it "significant as voicing an ill-founded discrimination of the wandering Seri from the inhabitants of Tiburon, as echoing persistent conception of Tiburon as a peninsula, and as summarizing the characteristics of the tribe recognized at the end of the last century." (W. J. McGee, "The Seri Indians," *17th Annual report of the Bureau of American Ethnology for the years 1895-1896*, pt. 1:83-84.)

184. Cerro Prieto.

185. The Tiburones and Tepocas were two of the three Serian-speaking groups distinguished by Europeans, the Guaymas being the third. The Seri peoples were conspicuous as the only major group of nonsedentary food collectors in Sonora, so reports of them emphasized primitive characteristics. See *Handbook* 10:230-49. A newer, more extensive analysis appears in Richard S. Felger and Mary B. Moser, *People of the Desert and Sea: An Ethnobotany of the Seri Indians* (Tucson: University of Arizona Press, 1985).

186. Bernard Fontana points out that Cortés erred in adopting the long-standing popular myth that the Seris walked or waded from Tiburon to the Sonoran mainland. Although it has never been possible to wade across the Infiernillo Straits, the persistence of that popular belief into this century led to the "Disaster on the Desert, 1905" that is reported in Neil B. Carmony and David E. Brown, eds., *Tales from Tiburon: An Anthology of Adventure in Seriland* (Phoenix: The Southwest Natural History Association, 1983), 57-84.

187. For this subsection and the remainder of Section 5, Cortés appears to rely principally upon the diary of Fray Garcés, as indicated in the concluding paragraph of the *Memorias*.

188. That is, the Pimas of the Gila River or the Upper Pimas. The term Pimas Altos embraces all northern Pimans, including Gileños, Pimas, Papagos, Sobas, Sobaipuris, etc.; all were residents of the so-called Pimería Alta, an area stretching northward from Magdalena and Caborca to the Gila River. The term distinguished that region from the Pimería Baja of central and southern Sonora, the homeland of other Piman-speaking Indians categorized as Pimas Bajos.

189. Extensive coverage of Pimas and Papagos appears in *Handbook*, vol. 10.

190. Now ordinarily categorized as Maricopas, these were indeed Yuman-speaking peoples. The Kaveltcadom are equated with the Cocomaricopas and the Opa with the Maricopas in Paul H. Ezell, *The Maricopas: An Identification from Documentary Resources*, Anthropological Papers of the University of Arizona, no. 61 (Tucson: University of Arizona Press, 1963). See also *Handbook* 10:71-85.

191. The Salt River.

192. Today written as Cocopa, these are another Yuman-speaking people. See *Handbook* 10:99-111.

193. Listed in *Handbook* 10:84, as Halyikwamai, another Yuman-speaking group ultimately incorporated with the Maricopa.

194. Given in *Handbook* 10:84, as Kahwan, another Yuman-speaking people ultimately incorporated with the Maricopa.

195. The Quechan, also known as Yuma; see *Handbook* 10:86-97.

196. The Mohave, northernmost and largest of the Yuman-speaking peoples of the lower Colorado River (*Handbook* 10:55-69).

197. The Halchidhoma are another of the Yuman-speaking groups that are now generally categorized as Maricopas. (*Handbook* 10:84). However, they are shown persisting as a distinct society in Marsha C. Kelly, "The Society That Did Not Die," *Ethnohistory* 19 (Summer, 1972): 261-65.

198. This reflects the perception of Fray Garcés concerning differences among subgroups of the Yuman languages.

199. For the story of Chief Salvador Palma and of the martyrdom of Fray Garcés and three other Franciscans at the hands of the Yumas, see John, *Storms Brewed in Other Men's Worlds*, 562-72, 605-609.

200. F. W. Hodge, annotating Indian nomenclature in the Coues edition of the Garcés diary (1:238, n. 11), was confident that these were the Panamint Indians, a Shoshonean-speaking people whose descendants are to be found in the vicinity of Death Valley (*Handbook* 10:118). A more recent interpretation is that Garcés applied the term to all of the people living along the Mohave River, in the San Gabriel and San Fernando valleys, along the upper reaches of the Santa Clara River, and in the Elizabeth Lake region, i.e., the Tataviam and Takic speakers. Yet another scholar in the same volume simply says that Garcés applied the term to all of the Serran peoples (*Handbook* 8:534, 570, 574). The moral for nonspecialists in the anthropology of Southern California appears to be that the science is still notably inexact.

201. Smith translated this as Gulf of California, but Pacific Ocean seems more plausible.

202. Hodge, annotating the Coues edition of the Garcés diary (1:269 n. 11), cannot trace the Cuabajais, but speculates that they were Shoshonean-speaking Paiutes. More recent scholars suggest that they were a distinct group, variously identified as Kitanemuk or Tataviam (*Handbook* 11:409-410).

203. Yokuts (*Handbook* 8:446-47.)

204. A sweathouse, for the sweatbath of both ritual and therapeutic function, which was common from the Mexican heartland northward at least as far as the Navajo and Apache. See Opler, *Apache Life-way*, 218-20. Hodge, in the Coues edition of the Garcés diary (1:284 n. 21), notes that the Spanish borrowed the word from the Nahuatl term for the sweathouse, *temazcalli*.

205. Cuñeil was probably a Kamia clan name. The terms Diegueño and Kamia have long been used to designate the closely related Yuman-speaking bands that occupied all the southern extreme of California in the era of Garcés; however, some anthropologists now designate those peoples by the terms Tipai and Ipai (*Handbook*, 8:608 and 592). Again, the nonspecialist can only note that this is an era of scholarship in which angels might fear to tread.

206. Santa Barbara Channel!

207. The Kamia, a Yuman-speaking people generally identified with the Diegueños. See *Handbook* 10:10, 100; and Hodge in the Coues edition of the Garcés diary, 1:166. The cautions about nomenclature in the preceding note on the Cuñeil apply equally to the Quemeyá.

208. Hodge, in the Coues edition of the Garcés diary (1:218 n. 26), equates the Jecuiche with the Cahuilla. *Handbook* 10:120, identifies Cahuilla as one of the Cupan languages, which were the southernmost Takic languages. See also *Handbook* 8:586.

209. San Gorgonio Pass, the boundary between the Shoshonean and Yuman speakers, according to Hodge in the Coues edition of Garcès, 1:205, n. 205.

210. In 1900, Hodge was able to find nothing more on the Jeniqueches than the fleeting mention of Garcés. The scholars of the new *Handbook of the American Indian* appear thus far to have had no better luck.

211. Garcés mentioned that the people called Cobaji by the Jamajabs were called Noches Colteches by the Noches (1:304) and also reported them to be bounded on the east by the Chemegué and on the west by the Noches (2:445.) *Handbook* 11:409-410, suggests that these were Kawaiisu, for whom Garcés recorded both the Mohave term "Cobaji" and the Yokuts term "Noches Colteches."

212. The Yavapai people of central and west-central Arizona spoke a dialect of an Upland Yuman language of which the other two major dialects were Walapai and Havasupai (*Handbook* 10:38-54). It is difficult to equate presently known names of Yavapai bands with those reported by Garcés, but the Jaquillapais appear to be the Walapai. See Hodge in Coues, *Garcés*, 1:231 n. 39).

213. A curious discrepancy is that Cortés lists Yavipais-abema, which does not appear in Garcés, but omits Yavipais-Jabesua, which figures importantly in Garcés, denoting the Havasupais to whom the priest was indebted for many favors. It appears that at some stage in the copying process "Jabesua" was garbled to "abema," providing another cautionary example of the risks inherent in manuscripts processed through many minds and hands.

214. For Walapai, see *Handbook* 10:25-37.

215. Hodge, in Coues, *Garcès* (1:225), suggests that the first four are all divisions of the Chemehuevi, and that the last are Paiutes, all now regarded as Shoshonean-speaking linguistic kinsmen. *Handbook* 11:393-94, identifies the Chemehuevis as a Southern Paiute subgroup whom Garcés recorded as Chemebet, Chemeguaba, Chemeguagua, and Chemegué, and notes that he also applied the terms Chemegué Cuajála and Chemegué Sevinta to Southern Paiute groups north of the Chemehuevi.

216. Here Cortés encountered some overlap in the reports of Garcés and of Domínguez-Escalante. The former reported that the Havasupai called some people living opposite them north of the Colorado "Payuches." He also called the same people "Payuchas" in reporting tales of them from the Yavapai and Quechans. Escalante reported "Payuchis", whom he classified as one of five "provinces" of the Ute nation, also calling them "Yuta Paiuches." These were, however, Southern Paiutes, not Utes (*Handbook* 11:393).

217. Hodge, in Coues, *Garcés* 2:404-406, nn. 9 and 13, was unable to identify

any of these; I find no persuasive identifications of these terms in subsequent publications.

218. The Yutas Zaguaganas, also reported as Sabuaganas, appear to be the people known today as Uncompahgre Utes (*Handbook* 11:366).

219. These are the Western Ute band now known as Timpanogots (*Handbook* 11:366).

220. Utah Lake.

221. In the Bolton edition of the Domínguez-Escalante diary, *Pageant in the Wilderness*, 189-92, 196-97, these appear as Yutas Barbarones.

222. *Handbook* 11:366, suggests that these were a Southern Paiute group, not another Ute people.

223. Apparently a reference to Bilaspur town and district of Madhyar-Pradesh State, located 205 miles northeast of Nagpur in Chattisgarh Plain, famous for ruins of a Hindu Kingdom of the eighth century A.D. (Jagdish Saran Sharm. *Encyclopaedia Indica* [New Delhi, 1975]).

224. Garcés refers to the exploration of Fray Juan de la Asunción through Sinaloa into present Arizona, a murky historical espisode treated at great length by Coues, 2:505-13. A recent, fuller analysis of the historiography of the Asunción episode appears in William K. Hartmann and Gayle Harrison Hartmann, "Juan de la Asunción, 1538: First Spanish Explorer of Arizona?," *The Kiva* 37(Winter, 1972):93-103.

225. The search for Quivira took both Coronado and Oñate from the Río Grande pueblos to the plains of present Kansas, where they found only the grass hut villages of Wichitan peoples in the area of the great bend of the Arkansas River.

226. Coues, *Garcés*, 1:280, identifies the Río de San Phelipe as the Kern River.

227. Coues argues persuasively (1:289, n. 30) that the great river of which the Noches informed Garcés was the San Joaquin.

## EPILOGUE

1. Manuel Toussaint, *Colonial Art in Mexico*, trans. by Elizabeth Wilder Weismann, 405-409; Fireman, *Spanish Engineers*, 133-36, 163-64.

2. The name Acordada applied to both a court with special jurisdiction concerning crimes of theft and to the jail that housed prisoners subject to its jurisdiction. The Casa de la Acordada occupied a choice tract now in the heart of Mexico City, running from the present corner of avenidas Bucareli and Juárez to Balderas; its large agricultural allotment, cultivated by prisoners, stretched southward from the court and jail complex (*Diccionario Porrua de Historia, Biografía y Geografía de México*, 3rd ed. [México: Editorial Porrua, 1964], 16). The area is now occupied principally by modern buildings; neither architectural histories of the city nor on-site investigations have yielded any indication that the barracks designed by Cortés were actually built.

3. José Cortés, Explicación General, México, June 28, 1801, and Cortés to Viceroy, June 29, 1801, in *Indiferentes de Guerra*, 463.A, folios 127-38; Planos 3375, 3376, 3377, 3378, 3379. Archivo General de la Nación, Mexico City.

4. Max L. Moorhead, "Spanish Deportation of Hostile Apaches, the Policy and the Practice," *Arizona and the West* 17(1975):211, 213, 215-16.

5. Fireman, *Spanish Engineers*, p.47.

6. Ramón Solís, *El Cádiz de las Cortés: La Vida en la Ciudad en los Años de 1810 a 1813*, 135-158.

7. The still elegant building, also known historically as the Pabellon de Ingenieros, is presently the Gobierno Militar, i.e., the headquarters of the military government of Cádiz.

8. A search of baptismal records at Cádiz yielded no entry for the Cortés infant, which may indicate that the stresses suffered by Doña Catalina late in her pregnancy resulted in loss of the child. However, the term "family" rather than "wife" does figure in the correspondence of fellow officers seeking assistance for Cortés after the pirate incident. Inquiry about burial records at the Cathedral in Murcia yielded the information that such records are retained in local parish churches, so that it would be necessary to know at which of the thermal baths Cortés was being treated when he died. It would presumably have been one of the four that have been important medical resources of the region of Murcia from ancient times to the present: Archena, Fortuna, Alhama, and Puebla de Mula, each recommended for specific disorders.

9. Ursula Lamb, "Martín Fernández de Navarrete Clears the Deck: The Spanish Hydrographic Office, (1809-24)," 5-9.

10. Juan Llabrés Bernal, *Breve Noticia de la Labor Científica del Capitán de Navío Don Felipe Bauzá y de Sus Papeles sobre América, 1764-1834*, 25-52; Ursula Lamb, "The London Years of Felipe Bauzá: Spanish Hydrographer in Exile, 1823-34" in *The Journal of Navigation*, 34:320-331.

11. Fray Pedro Font was the principal diarist of the overland expedition from Sonora to California led by Juan Bautista de Anza in 1775-76. Two versions of his diaries appear in Herbert Eugene Bolton, *Anza's California Expeditions*, the shortened diary in 3:202-307, and the complete diary comprising all of vol. 4.

12. Felipe Bauzá to Martín Fernández de Navarrete, Gibraltar, November 10, 1823; London, May 29 and July 26, 1824. Colección Navarrete at Abalos, of which this editor read photocopies in the Museo Naval, Madrid, through the gracious permission of D. Francisco Fernández de Navarrete, Marqués de Legarda, a descendant of Bauzá's distinguished colleague, who is now custodian of his papers.

13. Llabrés Bernal, *Breve Noticia de Don Felipe Bauzá*, 52-54.

14. Peel Papers, vol. 382, general correspondence, ff. 39 ff. British Library, Add. 40,562.

15. *Investigaciones sobre la antigua ciudad de Munda, hechas en España por el Ingeniero D. Domingo Velestá, a la solicitud de la Corte de Londres, para ilustracion de la Sociedad de Antiquarios Britanica, empleada en escribir la historia universal.*

16. Lamb, "London Years of Felipe Bauzá," 327.

17. An idea of the scope of the Bauzá collection can be gleaned from Pascual de Gayangos, *Catalogue of the Manuscripts in the Spanish Language in the British Museum*, 2:410-30.

18. Bauzá's copy of the Domínguez-Escalante diary, apparently in his own hand,

is in the Manuscripts Department of the British Library in Add. 17,560, a volume that also includes the diary of Fray Garcés. Add. 17,568, another of the Bauzá collection, also consists of copies of the Garcés and Domínguez-Escalante diaries. Clearly these were documents of great interest to Bauzá.

19. A. N. L. Munby, "The Formation of Phillipps Library between 1841 and 1872," 13.

20. *Biblioteca Phillippica: Catalogue of a Further Portion of the Manuscripts of the Late Sir Thos. Phillipps,* Wednesday, June 25, 1919, 68.; Maggs Brothers Catalog, 1955; Judy Credle, "Library Acquires Writings," *Arizona Daily Wildcat,* Tucson, December 9, 1955.

21. Edwin Black Brownrigg, *Colonial Latin American Manuscripts and Transcripts in the Obadiah Rich Collection: An Inventory and Index,* xiv-xvii.

22. Peter Force Papers, Series 8C, item no. 5.

23. William Goetzmann, *Exploration and Empire,* 288-92, 328.

24. A. W. Whipple et al., "Report upon the Indian Tribes," *Report of Explorations for a Railway Route,* Part III, 118-20. Goetzmann, p. 328, notes that Thomas Eubanks and W. W. Turner actually wrote the report that is generally attributed to Whipple.

25. W. J. McGee, "The Seri Indians" in BAE Annual Report, 17 (1895-96): 84.

26. Hodge in Coues, ed. *On the Trail of a Spanish Pioneer: The Diary and Itinerary of Father Garcés (Missionary Priest) in His Travels Through Sonora, Arizona, and California, 1775-1776,* 1:218, and 2:458.

27. Dolores A. Gunnerson, *The Jicarilla Apaches: A Study in Survival* (DeKalb: Northern Illinois University Press, 1974), 293.

# SELECT BIBLIOGRAPHY

Adams, Eleanor B., and Fray Angélico Chávez. *The Missions of New Mexico, 1776, A Description by Fray Francisco Atanasio Domínguez.* Albuquerque: University of New Mexico Press, 1956.

Baird, W. David. *The Quapaw Indians: A History of the Downstream People.* Norman: University of Oklahoma Press, 1980.

Barnes, Thomas C., Thomas H. Naylor, and Charles W. Polzer. *Northern New Spain, A Research Guide.* Tucson: University of Arizona Press, 1981.

Benavides, Adán, Jr. "Loss by Division: The Commandancy General Archive of the Eastern Interior Provinces." *The Americas* 43 (1986):203-206.

Bolton, Herbert Eugene, ed. and trans. *Athanase de Mézières and the Louisiana-Texas Frontier, 1768-1780.* 2 vols. Cleveland: Arthur H. Clark Co., 1914.

―――. *Pageant in the Wilderness: The Story of the Escalante Expedition to the Interior Basin, 1776, Including the Diary and Itinerary of Father Escalante Translated and Annotated.* Salt Lake City: Utah State Historical Society, 1950.

―――. *Anza's California Expeditions.* 5 vols. New York: Russell & Russell, 1966.

Brownrigg, Edwin Black. *Colonial Latin American Manuscripts and Transcripts in the Obadiah Rich Collection: An Inventory and Index.* New York Public Library, 1978.

Chapman, Carl H. *The Origin of the Osage Indian Tribe.* Osage Indians, vol. 3, Garland American Indian Ethnohistory Series. New York: Garland Publishing, 1974.

Chávez, Fray Angélico, trans., and Ted. J. Warner, ed. *The Domínguez-Escalante Journal.* Provo: Bringham Young University Press, 1976.

Cook, Warren L. *Flood Tide of Empire: Spain and the Pacific Northwest, 1543-1819.* New Haven: Yale University Press, 1973.

Coues, Elliott, ed. *History of the Expedition under the Command of Lewis and Clark to the Sources of the Missouri River, thence across the Rocky Mountains and down the Columbia River to the Pacific Ocean, performed during the years 1804-5-6.* 4 vols. New York: Francis P. Harper, 1893.

―――. *On the Trail of a Spanish Pioneer: the Diary and Itinerary of Francisco Garcés in His Travels through Sonora, Arizona, and California, 1775-1776.* 2 vols. New York: Francis P. Harper, 1900.

*Diccionario Porrua de Historia, Biografía y Geografía de México.* 3d ed. México: Editorial Porrua, 1964.

*Enciclopedia Universal Illustrada Europeo-Americana,* vols. 37 and 65. Madrid: Espasa-Calpe, 1918 and 1929.

Engstrand, Iris H. W. *Spanish Scientists in the New World: The Eighteenth Century Expeditions.* Seattle: University of Washington Press, 1981.

Ferg, Alan, ed. *Western Apache Material Culture: The Goodwin and Guenther Collections.* Tucson: University of Arizona Press, 1987.

Fireman, Janet R. *The Spanish Royal Corps of Engineers in the Western Borderlands: Instrument of Bourbon Reform, 1764 to 1815.* Glendale, Calif.: The Arthur H. Clark Co., 1977.

Fontana, Bernard L. "Apache Indians." In *The Reader's Encyclopedia of the American West,* edited by Howard R. Lamar, 34-37. New York: Thomas Y. Crowell, 1977.

Gálvez, Bernardo de. *Instructions for Governing the Interior Provinces of New Spain.*

Translated and edited by Donald E. Worcester. Berkeley: Quivira Society, 1951.

Galvin, John, ed. and trans. *A Record of Travels in Arizona and California, 1775-1776.* San Francisco: John Howell Books, 1965.

Gayangos, Pascual de. *Catalogue of the Manuscripts in the Spanish Language in the British Museum.* 2 vols. London: British Museum, 1877.

Goetzmann, William H. *Exploration and Empire: The Explorer and the Scientist in the Winning of the American West.* New York: Alfred A. Knopf, 1966.

Goodwin, Grenville. *Social Organization of the Western Apache.* Tucson: University of Arizona Press, 1969.

_____. *Western Apache Raiding and Warfare,* ed. by Keith H. Basso. Tucson: University of Arizona Press, 1971.

Griffen, William B. "The Compás: A Chiricahua Apache Family of the Late 18th and Early 19th Centuries." *The American Indian Quarterly* 7(1983):21-48.

_____. "Apache Indians and the Northern Mexican Peace Establishments." In *Southwestern Culture History: Collected Papers in Honor of Albert H. Schroeder,* edited by Charles H. Lange. Papers of the Archaeological Society of New Mexico 10:183-95. Santa Fe, 1985.

_____. *Apaches at War and Peace: The Janos Presidio, 1750-1858.* Albuquerque: University of New Mexico Press, 1988.

Gunnerson, Dolores A. *The Jicarilla Apaches: A Study in Survival.* DeKalb: Northern Illinois University Press, 1974.

*Handbook of North American Indians.* Vol. 8, *California* (1978); Vol. 9, *Southwest* (1979); Vol. 10, *Southwest* (1983); Vol. 11, *Great Basin* (1986). Washington, D.C.: Smithsonian Institution.

Hoijer, Harry. "The Position of Apachean Languages in the Athapaskan Stock." In *Apachean Culture History and Ethnology,* edited by Keith H. Basso and Morris E. Opler, Anthropological Papers of the University of Arizona, no. 21. Tucson: University of Arizona Press, 1971.

Holmes, Jack D. L. *Gayoso: The Life of a Spanish Governor in the Mississippi Valley, 1789-1799.* Baton Rouge: Louisiana State University Press, 1965.

Houck, Louis. *A History of Missouri.* 3 vols. Chicago: R. R. Donnelley, 1908.

Jackson, Donald, ed. *Letters of the Lewis and Clark Expedition with Related Documents, 1783-1854.* 2 vols. 2d ed. Urbana: University of Illinois Press, 1978.

Jenkins, Myra Ellen. "Spanish Colonial Policy and the Pueblo Indians." In *Southwestern Culture History: Collected Papers in Honor of Albert H. Schroeder,* edited by Charles H. Lange, Papers of the Archaeological Society of New Mexico 10:197-206. Santa Fe, 1985.

John, Elizabeth A. H. *Storms Brewed in Other Men's Worlds: the Confrontation of Indians, Spanish, and French in the Southwest, 1540-1795.* College Station: Texas A&M University Press, 1975; Lincoln; University of Nebraska Press, 1981.

_____. "Portrait of a Wichita Village, 1808." *Chronicles of Oklahoma* 60(Winter, 1982-83):412-37.

_____. "A Cautionary Exercise in Apache Historiography." *Journal of Arizona History* 25 (Autumn, 1984):301-15.

_____. "An Earlier Chapter of Kiowa History." *New Mexico Historical Review* 60 (October, 1985):379-97.

_____. "The Riddle of Mapmaker Juan Pedro Walker." In *Essays on the History of North American Discovery and Exploration*, edited by Stanley H. Palmer and Dennis Reinhartz. College Station: Texas A&M University Press, 1988.

_____. "Bernardo de Gálvez on Apaches: A Cautionary Tale for Gringo Historians." *Journal of Arizona History* 29 (Winter, 1988).

Kinnaird, Lawrence. *Spain in the Mississippi Valley, 1765-1794*. 3 vols. Annual Report of the American Historical Association for the Year 1945. Washington, D.C.: Government Printing Office, 1949.

Lamb, Ursula. "Martín Fernández de Navarrete Clears the Deck: The Spanish Hydrographic Office, 1809-24," Junta de Investigacoes Científicas Do Ultramar, Série Separatas 131. Coimbra: Centro de Estudos de Cartografia Antigua, 1980.

_____. "The London Years of Felipe Bauzá: Spanish Hydrographer in Exile, 1823-35," *Journal of Navigation* 34(September, 1981):319-40.

Llabrés Bernal, Juan. *Breve noticia de la labor científica del Capitán de Navio Don Felipe Bauzá y de sus papeles sobre América (1764-1834)*. Palma de Mallorca, 1934.

Lowery, Woodbury. *The Lowery Collection: A Descriptive List of Maps of the Spanish Possessions Within the Present Limits of the United States, 1502-1820*. Edited by Philip Lee Phillips. Washington, D.C.: Government Printing Office, 1912.

McGee, W. J. "The Seri Indians." Pt. 1 of *17th Annual Report of the Bureau of American Ethnology for the Years 1895-1896*, 1-344. Washington, D.C.: Government Printing Office, 1898.

Matson, Daniel S., and Albert H. Schroeder, eds. "Cordero's Description of the Apache–1796." *New Mexico Historical Review* 32(1957):335-56.

Moorhead, Max L. *The Presidio: Bastion of the Spanish Borderlands*. Norman: University of Oklahoma Press, 1975.

_____. "Spanish Deportation of Hostile Apaches, the Policy and the Practice." *Arizona and the West* 17 (1975):205-20.

Munby, A. N. L. "The Formation of Phillipps Library between 1841 and 1875." *Phillipps Study* 4. Cambridge: Cambridge University Press, 1956.

Nasatir, A. P. *Before Lewis and Clark: Documents Illustrating the History of the Missouri, 1785-1804*. 2 vols. St. Louis: St. Louis Historical Documents Foundation, 1952.

Opler, Morris Edward. *An Apache Life-way: The Economic, Social, and Religious Institutions of the Chiricahua Indians*. Chicago: University of Chicago Press, 1941.

Powell, Philip Wayne. *Tree of Hate: Propaganda and Prejudices Affecting United States Relations with the Hispanic World*. New York: Basic Books, 1971.

Sibley, John. "Historical Sketches of the several Indian tribes in Louisiana, south of the Arkansas river, and between the Mississippi and river Grande." In *American State Papers, Indian Affairs*, 1:721-25. Washington: Gales and Seaton, 1832.

Solís, Ramón. *El Cádiz de las Cortés: La Vida en la Ciudad en los Años de 1810 a 1813*. Cádiz: Silex, 1987.

Swanton, John R. *The Indians of the Southeastern United States*. Bureau of American Ethnology Bulletin No. 137. Washington, D.C.: Government Printing Office, 1946.

Toussaint, Manuel. *Colonial Art in Mexico*. Translated and edited by Elizabeth Wilder Weismann. Austin: University of Texas Press, 1967.

Whipple, Amiel W., Thomas Eubank, and William W. Turner. "Report upon the Indian Tribes." In *Report of Explorations for a Railway Route, near the Thirty-fifth Parallel of North Latitude, from the Mississippi River to the Pacific Ocean*, vol. 3, pt. 3:118-27. (U.S. Congress. House. 33rd Cong., 2d sess., 1855, Exec. Doc. no. 91).

# INDEX

Note: Indian peoples have been distinguished in main entries by use of bold type.

LaVergne, TN USA
14 September 2009
157720LV00002B/1/P